Community Health
Advocacy

Community Health Advocacy

Sana Loue, J.D., Ph.D., M.P.H.
Case Western Reserve University
Cleveland, Ohio

Linda S. Lloyd, Dr.P.H.
Alliance Healthcare Foundation
San Diego, California

and

Daniel J. O'Shea
San Diego County Office of AIDS Coordination
San Diego, California

Kluwer Academic / Plenum Publishers
New York, Boston, Dordrecht, London, Moscow

Library of Congress Cataloging-in-Publication Data

Loue, Sana.
  Community health advocacy/Sana Loue, Linda S. Lloyd, Daniel O'Shea.
    p.   cm.
  Includes bibliographical references and index.
  ISBN 0-306-47390-9
    1. Community health services. 2. Patient advocacy. 3. Community organizations. 4.
  Patient representatives. I. Lloyd, Linda S. II. O'Shea, Daniel, 1952– III. Title.

  R727.45 .L68 2002
  362.1'2—dc21
                                                                        2002027462

ISBN 0-306-47390-9

© 2003 Kluwer Academic / Plenum Publishers, New York
233 Spring Street, New York, New York 10013

http://www.wkap.nl

10 9 8 7 6 5 4 3 2 1

A C.I.P. record for this book is available from the Library of Congress

Printed in the United States of America

Preface

Health professionals are often confronted with situations that demand change including, for instance, a community's or population's inability to access adequate health care, or the need for a disease-specific prevention program where one does not exist, or a lack of understanding on the part of legislators as to the economic and noneconomic impacts of a particular disease or condition. In each such instance, advocacy may be required to move beyond the status quo. The form that the advocacy efforts take, however, may necessarily depend upon the specific issue at hand and the context in which the situation has arisen.

This text provides a foundation for the initiation of advocacy efforts and for the evaluation of their success. Chapters 1 and 2 provide a framework for advocacy efforts through an exploration of what it means to be, and to work with, a community, and how the needs of a particular community may be assessed.

It is critical to remember that, oftentimes, multiple strategies must be utilized simultaneously in order for advocacy efforts to succeed; accordingly, six chapters focus on specific strategies that can be utilized in an advocacy effort. Chapter 3, which addresses grassroots advocacy efforts, provides an overview of various theoretical models and numerous real-life examples of how grassroots efforts are organized. Chapter 4 continues to address community-wide advocacy issues through an exploration of the formation and development of coalitions. Chapters 5, 6, and 7 explore advocacy efforts in the more structured realms of legislatures, administrative agencies, and courts, while Chapter 8 focuses on media advocacy. Chapters 9 and 10 challenge the health professional engaging in advocacy efforts to establish a mechanism by which to judge the success of those efforts in terms of their outcomes and in terms of their solutions to the moral dilemmas that have been posed during the process. Each chapter concludes with one or more case studies, with discussion questions, and with a list of references.

We have drawn these chapters from our collective experience as researchers, health professionals, health advocates, and health program funders and from the many questions that have been posed to us in these capacities. This text is intended to provide both practical and theoretical guidance to health professionals and students who advocate for the protection, enhancement, and restoration of community health.

Acknowledgments

The authors gratefully acknowledge the helpful review and critique of earlier versions of this manuscript by Dr. Siran Koroukian, Dr. Ruth Lyn Riedel, and Nancy Mendez. Gary W. Edmunds and Nancy Mendez of Case Western Reserve University and Katherine Silver of Alliance Healthcare Foundation deserve praise and thanks for their time and diligence in locating needed materials. Mariclaire Cloutier of Kluwer Academic/Plenum Publishers deserves praise, as always, for her insightfulness and support.

Contents

Chapter One   **Defining Community** 1
Sociology 3
Psychology 6
Anthropology 7
Communitarian Philosophy 7
Public Health 9
Defining Community in Practice 10
Syringe Exchange in San Diego County,
1998–2001 10
Discussion Questions 13
References 14

Chapter Two   **Assessing Community Needs and
Framing Issues** 17
Definitions 17
What Is "Need"? 19
Conducting a Needs Assessment 19
Framing the Issue 29
Case Study 30
Discussion Questions 34
References 35

Chapter Three   **Organizing Community: Grassroots Activism** 37
Basic Concepts and Definitions 37
Theoretical Models of Community Organizing ... 40
Community Mobilization 43
Strategies for Community Organizing
and Mobilization 44
The Cycle of Organizing and Mobilization 48

Grassroots Advocacy in Action 50
ACT UP 56
Discussion Questions 58
References 59

Chapter Four   **Building Coalitions** 61
What Are Community Coalitions? 62
Strategies for the Formation of Multi-Level
    Coalitions 63
Coalitions in Action 69
A Coalition in Action: The Healthy Mothers,
    Healthy Babies Coalition 73
Discussion Questions 75
References 76

Chapter Five   **Legislative Advocacy** 77
The Legal System: An Overview 77
Legislatures 80
Legislative Advocacy in Action 84
Discussion Questions 89
References 90

Chapter Six   **Promoting Regulatory Change** 91
Administrative Agencies 91
Influencing Agency Rulemaking 100
Discussion Questions 101
References 102

Chapter Seven   **Using the Courts** 103
The Structure of the Court System 103
The Lawsuit As Advocacy 104
Advocacy in the Courts: Case Studies 107
Discussion Questions 116
References 117

Chapter Eight   **The Media** 119
Influence of the Media 119
Proactively Using the Media: Media
    Advocacy 121
Techniques and Strategies for Media
    Advocacy 124
Media Advocacy in Action: Case Study 133

	Discussion Questions	136
	References	136
Chapter Nine	**Evaluating the Advocacy Effort**	139
	The Evaluation Framework	140
	Media Advocacy	145
	Community-Wide Interventions	147
	Evaluating Syringe Exchange Advocacy Efforts	153
	Discussion Questions	155
	References	156
Chapter Ten	**Advocacy and Ethics**	159
	Advocacy and Ethics: Are the Two Compatible?	159
	Defining Community	160
	Community Consent	161
	Unanticipated Consequences	161
	Conflicts of Interest	162
	Discussion Questions	164
	References	165
Index	....	167

CHAPTER ONE

Defining Community

What is the city but the people?
(William Shakespeare, *Coriolanus*, III, i, 198)

Regardless of the discipline, an essential first step in any activity, be it research, provision of health services, health education, or health advocacy, is defining the target of the action. In public health programs, the community is generally referred to as the "target population." However, the term "target population" still refers to a group of individuals which has been aggregated for specific reasons. According to Webster's Third New International Dictionary (1993), "community" is defined as:

> (1) a body of individuals organized into a unit or manifesting usually with awareness some unifying trait: a. state, commonwealth; b. people living in a particular place or region; c. a monastic body or other unified religious body; d. an interacting population of different kinds of individuals constituting a society or association or simply an aggregation of mutually related individuals in a given location; e. a group of people marked by a common characteristic but living within a larger society that does not share that characteristic . . . (2) society at large . . . (3) common or joint ownership, tenure experience, or pertinence.

A review of the literature reveals an ongoing debate in the social sciences over what "community" means and the implications of those definitions in public health, social analysis, urban planning, and public policy, among other disciplines. Jewkes and Murcott (1998: 843) note that there "is a disjunction between the literatures of analytic social commentary . . . and to a certain extent health . . . and strategic declarations and policy documents of major national and international health institutions." The authors describe the community debate in the analytic social commentary literatures as "fiercely contested and hotly debated", while members of the health

1

fields "suggest that what is meant by community is self-evident" (Jewkes and Murcott, 1998: 843).

This chapter will briefly review how the term "community" is defined in different social science fields, with public health serving as the focus of the chapter and case study. In the past decade, there has been a greater emphasis in public health, and to some extent in health services, on "community-based" approaches to both individual and community health issues; for example, even though the desired outcome may be an individual behavior change (e.g., consistent use of condoms during sexual intercourse or a new, sterile syringe for every injection), the context of the message may have a broader community focus. Therefore, it is critically important to clearly understand how community has been defined, and who constitutes the community. Jewkes and Murcott (1998) would argue that it is equally important to know who defined the community and in what context. In their study of the operationalization of community participation in healthy cities projects in the United Kingdom, the authors found 28 different types of definition of community; definitions varied according to "... who was defining it, when, in what situation and for whom."

An increased discussion of the importance of involving communities in research (known as participatory action research, action research, or participatory research) has been welcomed by public health practitioners working at the community level. Green and Mercer (2001) call for a broad definition of "community," which would include not only groups affected by the research but also residents, practitioners, service agencies and policymakers. The authors believe that a broader definition of community is needed for there to be greater use of research findings in health practice and policy. Berlin (1997), a social policy planner, examined the ways people choose to live and how they define community. Communities as diverse as religious communities, neighborhoods consisting of single family homes, rural and urban communal living developments, and virtual communities were examined. Berlin notes that when "community" was used in the singular form, it was to indicate quality of life, that is, "the feeling of being together with others," while "communities" in its plural form referred to specific places or groups. She summarizes the definition of community which emerged from the interviews as something created by people with a common belief system or people working toward a common goal, with the neighborhood providing the most familiar context for community, based not upon likeness (associations or interest communities) but on diversity.

Of particular interest is the "virtual" community. The virtual community, a result of electronic communication technology, exists in cyberspace yet is made up of individuals who share feelings, life stories and experiences with people they will probably never meet. According to Berlin (1997), proponents of virtual communities feel that their type of community meets most of the standard criteria for defining "community," although other researchers do not agree that a virtual community is a "real" community. Berlin quotes Howard Rheingold, an author of several books on electronic communities and a firm believer that virtual communities are part of modern community, as noting that computer communications is a true grassroots phenomenon, started and maintained by people who want to share their interests. Rheingold also notes that many people who meet through the virtual community do meet in person, and some groups may meet on a regular basis outside the cyberspace community. Those who do not view virtual communities as true communities note that they generally lack the diversity found in real life since virtual communities are formed around a single interest. In electronic communications, when disagreement arises, individuals do not have to deal with the issue since they can remove the person from the list. This reduces people's exposure to those who are different from them, weakens the social skills needed for interaction with broader society and reinforces what some view as the "old" model of community, that is communities based on a single race or a single religion or a single interest. Participants of virtual communities view the ever-increasing diffusion of electronic technology throughout society as the means by which the diversity issue will be addressed. The field of study of virtual communities is still too young for judgement one way or the other, and the debate should continue to be thought-provoking.

SOCIOLOGY

Community Characteristics

According to Chekki (1990), the community is a key concept for understanding social life. In his introduction to community sociology, he quotes Wilkinson (1986, cited in Chekki, 1990:1), "As context, the community is not merely the background of the phenomena of central interest to sociology ... Far from being the mere geographical or territorial expression of larger systems in mass society, the community is an active ingredient in all of social life, a factor to be taken into account in attempting to understand whatever social processes and structures one finds in a given setting." While there is no one definition for the term community in sociology, modern communities are defined as "... a multidimensional concept" which are "primarily territorially-based open social systems." Chekki (1990) notes that contemporary communities, larger and with greater cultural complexity than in the past, are part of large national and international networks. One result is that community boundaries are harder to define, with individuals living in one place and working in another. Yet some sociologists posit that community as a social ecology, a holistic social organization and action field, does exist, even if the boundaries between local ecologies overlap and merge. Chekki summarizes this view by stating that " . . . community as an identifiable unit can exist despite its external linkages, and common interests based on sharing common space lead to collective action among people, when the need arises." (Chekki, 1990: 4).

Sinikka Dixon (1999) states that the term community has become an "omnibus" term, and as such is a difficult theoretical concept to address scientifically. The author provides a brief overview of how community has been viewed and defined over time within the field of sociology, noting that current trends tend to view community as an abstract, imagined community. According to Sinikka Dixon, the three elements found most consistently in the sociology literature as important features of community life are: (1) community is generally seen as delineated by a geographically, territorially, or spatially circumscribed area, (2) the members of a community are seen as bound together by a number of characteristics or attributes held in common (values, attitude, ethnicity, social class), and (3) the members of a community are engaged in some form of sustained social interaction. According to Sinnika Dixon (1999: 289), community is " . . . a concept which is at the interface of sociology and such other disciplines as anthropology, geography, politics, and urban planning." The author goes on to state that although the post-modern community is no longer seen as spatially bound, with groups functioning more like social networks, all members of society are in some way spatially bound and connected, even if only through the physical location of their home.

Communities of Circumstance

Marsh (1999) observes in his study of community participation in three different cities (two in Australia and one in England) that "communities of circumstance" can be formed when the right set of processes is present for community formation to take place. Marsh also believes, as does Sinnika Dixon, that people will have a spatial connection even if it is only through the physical location of their home. However, while individuals in geographically determined communities (e.g., voting districts, neighborhood planning councils) may not feel they are part of the community, community action may be required in order to address issues which will impact their neighborhood. Marsh studied what factors needed to be present for successful and sustained community development and participation to take place. He observed that the first step was for community formation, that is, that residents needed to create their sense of community based not on physical closeness of homes but through identification of shared values and interests. To do this, one needed to go beyond the concept that locality and community are linked, and recognize that communities of circumstance can result when there are processes which allow residents to identify common values and interests, and develop solutions to affect desired changes.

Some of the "circumstances" identified by Marsh as being necessary for the formation of a community of interest include: strong leadership, size and type of area (e.g., homes versus apartment buildings, rented versus owned), composition of the community, access to community workers who can assist the group, and the position of the local newspaper or other media toward community debate. March also noted that the "intensity of feelings generated" as part of the debate will contribute to the interest and willingness of residents to participate. Marsh examined types of community which formed in each of the three cities; in all three, interest communities formed along ideological orientations, and where ideological interest communities formed, ideology was as important as locality (1999).

As a result of advances in communication technology and increased travel and mobility of the population, one also encounters an ever-expanding list of "interest" communities, that is, groups of individuals associated with each other because of common interests rather than common geographical boundaries or locality. These interest communities may exist across geo-political boundaries thanks to current computer technology, and may encompass individuals from various ethnic, socioeconomic and political backgrounds. Of course, interest communities also exist within geographically-defined communities, and individuals may belong to a number of communities of both types.

Interest Communities

Some authors clearly distinguish between "community" and "association" (or interest community). For example, MacIver (1970: 30, originally published in 1936) defines a community as " ... any area of common life, village, or town or district, or country, or even wider area" which has some "characteristic of its own such that the frontiers of the area have some meaning." Examples of possible common characteristics include "manners, traditions, modes of speech," and reflect a "common life" the residents of this geographically-defined community share. An association, on the other hand, is "an organization of social beings . . . for the pursuit of some common interest or interests. It is a determinate social unity built upon common purpose." The reader will note that associations, which in 1936 were characterized by MacIver (1970: 31) as not being the equivalent of a community because a community is "something wider and freer . . . out of which associations arise . . . ," are now part of the definition for community in the Third New International Webster's dictionary. As noted by Chekki (1990) and Sinikka Dixon (1999), current trends in sociology now view associations as types of community, not just as components of a community.

PSYCHOLOGY

A common theme found in the psychology literature on community is that "sense of community" is a key research question, along with the identification and validation of elements which can serve as measurable indicators for this concept. According to Sagy, Stern and Krakover (1996), sense of community has assumed a central role in the field of community psychology in recent years. Sense of community has been defined as "a strong attachment that people may experience toward others based on factors such as where they live, where they work, where they go to school, or with which groups they affiliate (e.g., social, political, religious, clinical treatment, cultural)"(Davidson & Cotter, 1993: 59). In 1976, McMillan defined sense of community as "a feeling that members have of belonging, a feeling that members matter to one another and to the group, and a shared faith that members' needs will be met through their commitment to be together." (McMillan & Chavis, 1986).

McMillan and Chavis (1986) identified four elements which make up the sense of community construct: membership, influence, integration and fulfillment of needs, and shared emotional connection. The authors state that these elements are equally applicable to both geographically and relationally defined communities; relational communities are those that do not have a reference to location, but result from other relationships among the members. In the sociology literature, relational communities were called interest communities. The authors identify various areas of application of this theoretical framework, stating that a clear and empirically validated definition of sense of community can lay the foundation for planning for community services, as well as community organizing and advocacy. The authors provide planning for community treatment programs for the mentally disabled and mentally ill as an example of this. An understanding of sense of community helped develop strategies that allowed the therapeutic benefits of community to be developed within group homes and assisted with the integration of the homes into the surrounding communities.

The debate in the community psychology field is as lively as that noted in the field of sociology, with discussion focusing on a general loss of a sense of community in modern society and the underlying reasons for this loss. A recurring theme in the community psychology literature is understanding how sense of community develops in modern communities, which are increasingly relational or interest communities, and the identification of new reference points which will provide a greater understanding of modern community (Glynn, 1986). In his summary of research on neighborhood and sense of community, Glynn notes that social network researchers support a social network analytical framework as being more appropriate for examining the concept of community.

ANTHROPOLOGY

Traditional anthropological studies have tended to use geographical and familial definitions for defining community, although street ethnographers use both locality and relational definitions for their work. Stryker (1989) describes injection drug use behaviors as a social phenomena due to mutual dependence created by the illegal nature of the drug use. Des Jarlais, Friedman, Sotheran, and Stoneburner (1988) note that an understanding of the social organization of the injection drug use subculture helps researchers and public health practitioners to appreciate the economic forces and interpersonal relationships involved in the sharing of drug injection equipment, which resulted in the rapid spread of HIV among injection drug users (IDUs) in New York City. When reviewing the literature on street ethnography of injection drug use, both sociologists and anthropologists have identified IDUs as a unique community; some consider it a deviant subculture, with shared values, a common language, and rules for allocating status within the group.

COMMUNITARIAN PHILOSOPHY

Communities and Individuals

Another perspective on community comes from the literature on communitarianism. Etzioni (1995) describes the two leading schools of thought as those that view communitarian philosophy as a source for reform for contemporary liberalism while others emphasize the ways in which communitarian philosophy provides a different approach to political theory. While communitarians recognize individual rights and freedom, they also recognize that individual freedom derives from a broader context of obligations resulting from communal attachments and responsibilities. Etzioni views individuals and communities as "... constitutive of one another, and their relationship is, at one and the same time, mutually supportive and tensed." According to Etzioni (1995), changes in this balance between individual and community will undermine the benefits which accrue from a properly balanced relationship. The author defines community as a "web of social relations that encompass shared meanings and above all shared values," noting that people are members of several communities, with communities "nested, each within a more encompassing one" (Etzioni, 1995: 24). For example, one's neighborhood is part of a larger suburb or city, which in turn is part of a larger regional unit. These geographic communities then intersect with communities which may be ethnically, professionally, or special interest-based, among other possible associations.

Public Communities

Fowler (1995) notes the diversity and disagreement with definitions for community, with some researchers favoring a more "public" definition of community. Fowler, favoring the public definition, identifies three kinds of community in current American political thought: (1) communities of ideas (for example, participatory democratic [broad-based decision-making through face-to-face discussions] and republican political [emphasis on public virtue and public-spiritedness] models), (2) communities of crisis (for example, the "earth community" and other groups aiming to overcome social and ecological crises), and (3) communities of memory (for example, religious and traditional ideas of community). These three kinds of community reflect, according to the author, the principal concepts of community today, as well as the lack of consensus on what community means. Fowler notes that intellectual discussion has focused on the first type of community, that of the relative merits and even existence of participatory and republican communities, while communities of crisis form from current events rather than intellectual discussion. However, underlying both the theoretical and the crisis-driven types of community are public concepts of what community is, or was; this is the community of memory which derives from well-established belief systems, primarily those of tradition and religion.

PUBLIC HEALTH

Public health practitioners bring their own definitions of community to this lively and diverse discussion of what community is, and what community means. Community is oftentimes defined through disease status (e.g., presence or absence of disease; chronic or acute disease), or the presence of risk factors for disease (e.g., high blood pressure, overweight, alcohol and drug use patterns). These broad "communities" are generally broken into smaller groups which may be created by ethnicity, age, or gender. Other common ways of defining community found in public health programs include rural vs. urban, inner city vs. suburban, sexual orientation, socioeconomic status, and immigration status. These groupings may assist in detecting significant differences in disease rates between the groups, differences in cultural interpretations of the disease or risk factor, or differences in service utilization rates. Members of these "communities" may not know they are members until they receive a specific medical diagnosis, or they may explicitly reject being classified in the group. However, these groupings are common in the published literature and are part of the framework in which service providers and public health practitioners conduct their work.

MacQueen and colleagues (2001) describe the results of a study to assess whether "community" was defined in similar ways across diverse groups. The authors asked African Americans in Durham, North Carolina, gay men in San Francisco, California, injection drug users in Philadelphia, Pennsylvania, and HIV vaccine researchers across the United States what the word "community" meant to them, and then identified common themes across the responses. The authors found a common definition of community: a group of people with diverse characteristics who are linked by social ties, share common perspectives, and engage in joint action in geographical locations or settings (MacQueen, McLellan, Metzger, Kegles, Strauss, Scotti, Blanchard, and Trotter, 2001: 1929). However, they also found differences in how the four groups experienced community. These different experiences of each group led to an emphasis on different elements of the core definition. For example, for the gay men in San Francisco, a shared history and perspective was the dominant theme, followed by a sense of identity with the location; for African Americans in Durham and injection drug users in Philadelphia, locus was the principal element for community, followed by joint action and social ties. MacQueen and colleagues (2001: 1935) call for the use of "multiple models of collaboration in public health research and program" because of the variation in experience of community across different settings.

In the medical research field, participants must meet clearly defined inclusion criteria, for example in a clinical trial for a new drug to treat HIV infection, or they will be ineligible for the study. The clinical trial in effect creates a "community" of individuals through a well-defined medical status, although they may have little else in common. Individuals in a health system may constitute a community, and they may develop a strong sense of community within the health system as a result of time spent in the system as a patient, a volunteer or family member of a patient. In the field of public health, communities are geographically as well as relationally defined. For example, in an epidemiological study of exposure to environmental contaminants and a disease(s), clearly defined physical boundaries within which the exposure took place would be necessary in order to assess the relationship between the exposure and the disease(s) attributed to it. However, a health education program targeting a specific ethnic group may need to rely on relational communities such as churches, social clubs, or the workplace, to successfully reach the population.

DEFINING COMMUNITY IN PRACTICE

How individuals associate with the broader society has changed over the past fifty years; researchers need to rethink how community is defined and how community participation in research studies, community-based programs and advocacy can be effectuated. If individuals participate in many different communities which are both locality- and relational-based, how do program planners, community organizers, and policy makers, among the many groups which depend upon "community" to carry out their responsibilities, reach their constituents or target population? How do they know if they have successfully reached the community they hoped to reach? Clearly defining the objectives of the program, the target population and the ways the members of the community might self-associate will enable program planners or community organizers to identify the types of communities they need to outreach to, outreach strategies for each type of community and outcomes appropriate for each community. The case study that follows describes how community was defined for a public education and advocacy campaign in support of clean syringe exchange as part of a comprehensive harm reduction program for injection drug users.

SYRINGE EXCHANGE IN SAN DIEGO COUNTY, 1998–2001

All information for the following case study is from the Alliance Healthcare Foundation grant files for the campaign.

Background

In the State of California, possession of hypodermic syringes without a prescription from a physician is against the law under state drug paraphernalia laws. As a result, clean syringe exchange programs have been considered to be illegal activities, with outreach workers and individuals exchanging syringes under threat of arrest for possession of drug paraphernalia. In January 2000, Assembly Bill 136 (AB136) was enacted, allowing local jurisdictions to declare medical states of emergency under which clean syringe exchange programs can legally function. It is important to understand that AB136 only provides legal protection to the outreach workers running the program, not to the individuals exchanging used syringes for clean ones. For policy planners and community advocates, the overwhelming preponderance of research clearly demonstrating the effectiveness of clean syringe exchange programs in reducing the transmission of blood-borne diseases such as HIV and hepatitis C was confirmed, once again, in March, 2000, by the U.S. Surgeon General. Dr. David Satcher, the U.S. Surgeon General was asked to summarize the published scientific literature by Congress, and in his report stated, "Syringe exchange programs as part of a comprehensive HIV prevention strategy are an effective public health intervention that reduces the transmission of HIV and does not encourage the use of illegal drugs" (United States Surgeon General, 2000).

Public Education and Advocacy Campaign for Clean Syringe Exchange

A local healthcare foundation undertook a public education and advocacy campaign to generate community support for the declaration of a medical state of emergency in San Diego County, California, a necessary first step to establishing a legal program under AB136, and subsequent implementation of a clean syringe exchange program. This campaign took place over a three-year period, during which time it was necessary to revise and review the definition of community as the campaign progressed.

Phase 1 was intended to increase general community support for syringe exchange by addressing common misconceptions of the need for such a program and expanding in the public's mind the definition of "who" the affected community is. The target community was defined at the start of Phase 1 both geographically and relationally. The campaign, while providing information to the general population, targeted registered voters through specific messages which formative research (also known as formative evaluation) indicated resonated with voters, e.g., cost of preventable infections to the taxpayer, unintended victims (e.g., pediatric AIDS cases, partners of injection drug users), significant discrepancies in infection rates by ethnicity. To reach voters at their place of residence, a series of advertisements was placed in neighborhood newspapers throughout the county and ethnic-specific newspapers or magazines; formative research demonstrated that many people read their neighborhood or ethnic-specific newspaper more than the large newspaper which covers the county. Six billboard spaces strategically located throughout the county were purchased to remind people of the campaign slogan and the foundation's website where additional information could be found, on their commute to and from work. The same series of newspaper ads was also placed in a general interest arts and culture magazine with county-wide distribution.

A series of radio spots, in both English and Spanish, which mirrored the newspaper ads was also developed. Radio spot time was purchased on specific stations in order to reach the community of individuals who identified with the type of programming. For example, time was purchased on radio stations with a more conservative audience given the conservative nature of San Diego County residents. Research also demonstrated that a large number of Spanish speakers rely on the radio rather than print media for information, so a greater emphasis was placed on the Spanish-language spots rather than Spanish-language print material.

The third communication strategy was interpersonal, that is, presentations to community groups or one-on-one presentations with elected officials. The community groups were both geographically-defined (e.g., community planning groups) or relationally-defined (e.g., service organizations such as Kiwanis and Rotary, professional organizations such as the Police and Firefighters Associations, social action committees of churches, and disease-specific groups such as HIV/AIDS service providers). Because the police department would be critical to the initiation and success of the program, e.g., refraining from confiscating syringes during a search, presentations were given on an individual basis to active and retired senior police and sheriff's department staff.

In Phase 2, the definition of community was narrowed from registered voters and elected officials throughout San Diego County to that of residents of the City of San Diego, the council members representing the eight districts which make up the City of San Diego, and community leaders identified in Phase 1. The radio spots were aired a second time to remind the general population of the issue. Presentations to community groups continued but not at the same level as during Phase 1. This narrowing of the definition of the community to be reached enabled the advocacy team to conduct highly targeted outreach and to refine messages to address the specific concerns of local decision-makers. Communities that were not reached to the extent desired in Phase 1, such as business and religious leaders, were re-assessed and new strategies were developed to achieve outreach objectives. Outreach to the police and sheriff's departments was not continued, although information was provided as requested to the Police Officers Association. The campaign team worked with local city council members to respond to questions from the police department. One relational community successfully reached during Phase I was that of individuals who had tested positive for hepatitis C, and whose infection was not necessarily due to injection drug use. Many of these individuals, including those with asymptomatic as well as those with active disease, spoke publicly at city council meetings for the first time about their disease, and called on city officials to allow comprehensive harm reduction strategies, including clean syringe exchange to function.

Results of the Public Education and Advocacy Campaign

In November 2000, the San Diego City Council declared a medical state of emergency and requested that the City Manager convene a task force to (1) examine the need for clean syringe exchange in the City of San Diego and (2) design an appropriate program for City Council consideration (City of San Diego Clean Syringe Exchange Program Task Force Final Report, June 12, 2001; http://www.alliancehf.org). In November 2001, the City Council voted again to declare a medical state of emergency and authorized the start-up of a one-year, privately-funded pilot clean syringe exchange program (Alliance Healthcare Foundation, personal communication, November 2001).

DISCUSSION QUESTIONS

1. You are the Director of Health Promotion at a community clinic which serves an ethnically diverse population. You have been asked by your supervisor to design a community advocacy program for the prevention of HIV and other sexually transmitted diseases of importance to men who have sex with men (MSM). Describe and justify how you would define the community(ies) you should target in your campaign.

2. You are employed by a nonprofit organization that provides services to the city's homeless population. You have been asked to determine which needs of the homeless population should be given priority

in allocating funding. Explain how you will define the homeless community in this context.

REFERENCES

Berlin, S. (1997). *Ways We Live*. Gabriola Island, British Columbia, Canada: New Society Publishers.

Chekki, D.A. (1990). Introduction: Main currents and new directions in community sociology. In D.A. Chekki (Ed.), *Research in Community Sociology, Vol. 1: Contemporary Community: Change and Challenge* (pp. 1–22). Greenwich, Connecticut: Jai Press Inc.

Davidson, W.B., & Cotter, P.R. (1993). Psychological sense of community and support for public school taxes. *American Journal of Community Psychology, 21*, 59–66.

Des Jarlais, D.C., Friedman, S.R., Sotheran, J.L., & Stoneburner, R. (1988). The sharing of drug injection equipment and the AIDS epidemic in New York City. In Needle Sharing Among Intravenous Drug Abusers: National and International Perspectives.

Etzioni, A. (1995). Old chestnuts and new spurs. In A. Etzioni (Ed.), *New Communitarian Thinking: Persons, Virtues, Institutions, and Communities* (pp. 16–34). Charlottesville, VA: University Press of Virginia.

Fowler, R.B. (1995). Community: reflections on definition. In A. Etzioni (Ed.), *New Communitarian Thinking: Persons, Virtues, Institutions, and Communities* (pp. 88–95). Charlottesville, VA: University Press of Virginia.

Glynn, T.J. (1986). Neighborhood and sense of community. *Journal of Community Psychology, 14*, 341–352.

Green, L.W., & Mercer, S.L. (2001). Can public health researchers and agencies reconcile the push from funding bodies and the pull from communities? *American Journal of Public Health, 91*, 1926–1929.

Jewkes, R., & Murcott, A. (1998). Community representatives: Representing the "community"? *Social Science and Medicine, 46*, 843–858.

MacIver, R.M. (1970). *On Community, Society and Power. Selected Writings.* L. Bramson, Ed. Chicago: The University of Chicago Press.

MacQueen, K.M., McLellan, E., Metzger, D.S., Kegeles, S., Strauss, R.P., Scotti, R., Blanchard, L., Trotter II, R.T. (2001). What is community? An evidence-based definition for participatory public health. *American Journal of Public Health, 91*, 1929–1938.

Marsh, G. (1999). The community of circumstance — a tale of three cities: Community participation in St. Kilda, Knox, and Lewisham. In D.A. Chekki (Ed), *Research in Community Sociology, Vol. 9: Varieties of Community Sociology* (pp. 65–88). Greenwich, CT: Jai Press.

McMillan, D.W., & Chavis, D.M. (1986). Sense of community: A definition and theory. *Journal of Community Psychology, 14*, 6–23.

Sagy, S., Stern, E., & Krakover, S. (1996). Macro- and microlevel factors related to sense of community: The case of temporary neighborhoods in Israel. *American Journal of Community Psychology, 24*, 657–675.

Sinikka Dixon, A.L. (1999). The hidden community: Spatial dimensions of urban life. In D.A. Chekki (Ed.), *Research in Community Sociology, Vol. 9: Varieties of Community Sociology* (pp. 287–308). Greenwich, CT: Jai Press.

Stryker, J. (1989). IV drug use and AIDS: Public policy and dirty needles. *Journal of Health Politics, Policy and Law, 14*, 719–740.

United States Surgeon General (2000, March 17). Evidence-based findings on the efficacy of syringe exchange programs: An analysis from the Assistant Secretary for Health and Surgeon General of the scientific research completed since April 1998. http.//www.harmreduction.org/surgreview.html.

Webster's Third New International Dictionary (1993). Springfield, Massachusetts: Merriam-Webster.

CHAPTER TWO

Assessing Community Needs and Framing Issues

CLIENT INTAKE
A. White, 42 years old
B. Talks fast
C. Air Force veteran
D. Homeless since 1986
E. Has no income
F. Admits he is a paranoid schizophrenic
(Burns, 1998: 67)

What are needs assessments and why are they used? The definition varies in detail, but simply put, needs assessments are tools that are used to gain knowledge about a particular group. Just as the definition varies, so do the methods that can be used to conduct a needs assessment. This chapter will focus on what needs assessments are, when to use them, and the methods to choose from.

DEFINITIONS

Reviere and colleagues (1996) state that needs assessments are tools designed to identify what a particular group of persons lacks to achieve more satisfactory lives. The authors discuss the importance of defining the term "need," and what it means in the context of the assessment process. They note underlying assumptions that existing data will either clearly show what the need is, or that people will be able to answer the question of what they need, with the researcher just asking the question. The authors challenge these assumptions in their discussion of what "need" and "want" mean, by emphasizing the importance of understanding the community meaning of need, and what happens when the community and service providers disagree over what is needed, or even how to meet a mutually identified need.

Witkin and Altschuld (1995) broadly define needs assessment as a systematic set of procedures undertaken for the purpose of setting priorities based on identified needs, and making decisions about program or organizational improvement and the allocation of resources. The needs assessment seeks to identify discrepancies (needs), examine the nature of and causes for the discrepancy, and set priorities for action. Kaufman (2000) defines a needs assessment as identifying gaps between current results and desired (or required) ones, and explicitly notes that needs are not insufficient levels of resources, means or methods; rather, a need only refers to the gap between "current and desired results." Once the gaps have been identified, they can be ranked in priority order for resolution based on the cost to meet the need as compared to the cost of ignoring it. Kaufman (2000) states that most needs assessments described in the literature focus not on gaps in results, but on gaps in processes or resources. The problem with this, according to Kaufman, is that when gaps in resources are the focus (e.g., training, computer equipment), the end result is less clearly defined and sometimes even ignored, and the solution treats the symptoms rather than the causes. Therefore, it is necessary to first define the gap in current and desired results, then the means or resources needed to reduce the gap.

The National Council of La Raza (NCLR) defines community needs assessment as "a systematic process designed to determine the current status and unmet needs—sometimes, both the present and future needs—of a defined population group or geographic area with regard to a specified program or subject area" (1995: 44). NCLR developed a guidebook for HIV Prevention Community Planning Board members to design comprehensive HIV prevention plans; this process, a Centers for Disease Control and Prevention (CDC) mandate for areas receiving CDC funds for HIV prevention programs, is to assure that the planning process includes diverse community involvement. The authors note that for a community needs assessment to be both valid and credible, it must include the following components: (1) broad agreement on the purposes, focus and scope of the needs assessment, (2) a multi-disciplinary assessment team that includes individuals with expertise in community assessment procedures, knowledge about strategies relevant to the issue under study, and members of the affected population group(s), (3) a process for regular review and input by community representatives, (4) a study design that makes effective use of primary and secondary data, (5) a plan for using the results, and (6) a realistic study design, time frame and resource allocation (NCLR, 1995).

Reviere and colleagues (1996) summarize definitions of needs assessments as "a measure of how much of what is needed" (York, 1982, cited in Reviere, et al. 1996: 6), "a process of ordering and prioritization of community needs" (McKillip, 1987, cited in Reviere et al., 1996: 6), and "a systematic process of collection and analysis as inputs into resource allocation decisions with a view to discovering and identifying goods and services the community is lacking in relation to the generally accepted standards, and for which there exists some consensus as to the community's responsibility for their provision" (United Way of America, 1982, cited in Reverie et al., 1996: 6). However needs assessment is defined, central elements include a measure of something that is below commonly accepted standards (the need or gap), a community identification of the need or gap as being important, and an ability to positively affect the need or gap.

WHAT IS "NEED"?

Without a clear understanding of how the term "need" is defined in the context of any needs assessment, it will be difficult to design and implement an assessment process that will provide data that can be used for the purpose for which is was intended. Witkin and Altschuld (1995: 5) define a need as being a discrepancy or gap between "what is" and "what should be." Reviere and colleagues (1996: 5) define need as "a gap-between the real and ideal conditions-that is both acknowledged by community values and potentially amenable to change." The authors define values as "ideas about what is good, right, and desirable," and note that values are central to judgement and behavior. The authors call on researchers and participants to discuss their own values openly throughout the needs assessment process, beginning with planning through data analysis and interpretation. The authors also describe three components of "need," all three of which must be present for a need to be classified as such: first, there must be a gap between the real and ideal conditions in a community, with narrowing the gap a goal; second, the gap must be perceived and acknowledged as a need by the community; and third, the gap must be amenable to change, or if not amenable to change, it must have conditions which are modifiable.

CONDUCTING A NEEDS ASSESSMENT

There are several elements to consider during the needs assessment process. The first step is to clearly define the target population whose needs will be assessed; the target population can be defined using geographic, social or health characteristics, and demographic character-istics. Once the population has been identified, the research question or questions the needs assessment is to answer can be refined and precisely stated (Berkowitz, 1996a). These two elements must be in place before the needs assessment can be designed since data collection methods will de-pend upon the population being targeted and the type of data needed to answer the question. For example, mailing a standardized question-naire to low-income immigrant family households may not be appro-priate if the population has low literacy levels or if the individuals are not used to filling in surveys. This method could result in a low re-turn rate and lead to questions as to the reliability and validity of the data.

The needs assessment team will need to determine the type and scope of needs to investigate (Berkowitz, 1996a). Some needs assessments are highly specific, gathering information on a single issue (e.g., low-income housing) or from a very specific group in the population (e.g., injection drug users), while others may address a wide range of issues (e.g., access to medications, supportive health and social services, transportation, and housing for low-income elderly) or a larger population (e.g., access to den-tal health services statewide). Unless funding is unlimited, needs assess-ment processes must balance the number of categories for which data are collected and the scope of the assessment.

Reviere and colleagues (1996) list common problems found in needs assessments: sampling problems, failure to collect data that measure the desired components of need, and the use of methods that are inappro-priate or inadequate to justify the conclusions reached. The authors also note that many agencies involved in needs assessments view the assess-ment as the final product, rather than as a means to make changes or modifications in the ways services are provided or to advocate for new policies. For example, most needs assessments reviewed by Kimmel (1977, in Reviere, 1996) did not include a discussion of program or policy impli-cations of the findings, and Thompson (1981, in Reviere, 1996) found little to support the belief that needs assessment results contributed to informed decision-making.

Needs Assessment Process

A three-stage needs assessment process (Witkin and Altschuld, 1995) will be described in this section. These stages are not the only way to describe the process, but they do provide a useful framework to initiate planning for the assessment.

Stage 1: Pre-Assessment

The pre-assessment stage includes all preliminary planning and background research activities (Witkin and Altschuld, 1995). This is a key part of the needs assessment process since during this stage, the needs assessment team will need to ensure that appropriate stakeholders are part of the process, develop clear goals and objectives for the needs assessment, develop the research questions, and examine existing information about the target group and/or the issues. During the pre-assessment stage, the data to be collected, sources for the data, methods to collect the data, data analysis plans, and procedures to use the findings should be identified and documented. Points to consider include the budget for the needs assessment, the cost of collecting and analyzing the data, identification of special needs of the target population that may affect data collection methods, and project timelines.

Stage 2: Assessment

The focus of this stage of the needs assessment is data collection and analysis. After the needs assessment team has identified the research questions, the data needed to answer them and appropriate methods for collecting the data, the second stage of the process begins with the development of the data collection instruments. These instruments might include forms for data abstraction from existing databases, survey instruments and structured interview guides for focus groups or individual interviews. According to Witkin and Altschuld (1995), analysis of the data should highlight differences in magnitude of need, not just those differences which are statistically significant.

Triangulation, the use of different, independent approaches to address research questions, strengthens the basis for conclusions drawn from the study since different data sources, theoretical perspectives and methods are used simultaneously (Berkowitz, 1996b). Lasker and colleagues (1997) note that the results of community health assessments will be more robust if data are aggregated from multiple sources–for example, quantitative data derived from surveys and administrative databases and qualitative information drawn from community meetings, interviews, and focus groups—and analyzed from multiple perspectives. Elliot, Quinless and Parietti (2000) describe a grassroots neighborhood assessment process in which both qualitative and quantitative methods were used to identify perceived strengths, weaknesses, and opportunities in the neighborhood; the self-reported demographics of local residents and clients of a neighborhood collaborative (a local Church, the school affiliated with the Church,

and the "Club"—a social and welfare service provider); service priorities and needs of residents and collaborative clientele; and directions
for financially sound strategic planning, effective community organizing
and efficient communications. The needs assessment, community-driven
and implemented, included surveys of residents and users of the collaborative's services, focus group interviews with residents, teachers, and
Club service providers, and a review of the 1990 census data for the
area.

Stage 3: Post-Assessment

This phase is the action phase, during which the data analysis results are put into action. During post-assessment, determining how the
information can be used and developing strategies for dissemination of
results and, where applicable, new programs or policies to address the
needs identified through the process takes place. Use of findings from
the needs assessment will only occur if action plans are developed and
there is a commitment on the part of all groups involved to implement the
action plans. Many authors note that most needs assessments do not include this critical component; Witkin and Altschuld (1995) cite a study
of 125 published needs assessments in which fewer than half discussed
the priorities identified. The authors provide five tasks that should be
part of every post-assessment phase: (1) set priorities on the needs,
(2) select solution strategies to meet the needs, (3) propose an action plan
to implement the solutions, (4) evaluate the quality of the total needs assessment, and (5) prepare written reports and oral briefings (Witkin and
Altschuld, 1995). It is interesting to note that preparation of the written
report follows development and implementation of the action plan, reinforcing the importance of actually using the findings from the needs assessment to address the issues investigated through the needs assessment
process.

Needs Assessment Methods

As noted by several authors (Berkowitz, 1996a; NCLR, 1995; Witkin
and Altschuld, 1995), triangulation of research methods can provide a
stronger basis for conclusions derived from the needs assessment. This
section will examine recommended methods that might be employed in
a needs assessment, with references for the reader should more detailed
information on a specific method be desired.

Review of Existing Data Sources

Obtaining social, economic and demographic information on the group or geographic area to be targeted by the needs assessment is an essential first step in the pre-assessment stage of a needs assessment. This information can be obtained from a number of sources such as governmental agencies (e.g., U.S. Census Bureau, the Centers for Disease Control and Prevention [CDC], the Environmental Protection Agency [EPA], Housing and Urban Development), city, regional and state health and human services agencies (e.g., health and social welfare departments, local housing agencies), education systems (e.g., public school systems), and local service providers (e.g., community clinics, social service agencies, non-profit housing agencies, treatment and recovery providers). When using existing data sources, it is important to keep in mind that the data were collected for a purpose other than the needs assessment and data inferences should be drawn with care.

Existing data sources may consist of established databases which can be used for secondary data analysis, such as disease surveillance data routinely collected by the health department, state or national level disease surveillance data reports, census data, reports of survey or other assessment activities conducted in schools (e.g., the CDC-sponsored "Youth Risk Behavior Survey" conducted in middle and high schools throughout the U.S.), program evaluation reports, and reviews of the scientific literature. Summaries of data collected during the pre-assessment stage may serve to provide a broader context for the needs assessment, further refine research questions, and support future program and policy activities.

Data Collection Methods

Interviewing is the most commonly used method of data collection. There are two types of interviews, individual and group, each with advantages and disadvantages. Each type will be described in this section. The first three types of interviewing (informal, unstructured, and semi-structured) are all qualitative research methods. The last type of interviewing, structured interviews (e.g., surveys), is a quantitative research method.

Individual Interviews. The following classification and descriptions of types of individual interview are taken from Bernard (1994); however, all four types of interview are described by other social scientists, although they may use other terms. The four types of interviews range from completely unstructured to very structured formats.

Informal interviews (called "friendly conversations" by Spradley, 1988), a qualitative research method, can be described as informal conversations that the researcher does not guide or direct in any manner. This type of interviewing is most commonly undertaken when the researcher is just starting fieldwork. It is useful for getting to know residents and to identify additional topics of relevance to the research question.

Unstructured interviews (known as "ethnographic interviews" [Spradley, 1988], "key informant interviews" [Pelto and Pelto, 1987] or "guided interviews" [Grbich, 1999]), also a qualitative research method, can be described as interviews in which both the researcher and the informant know that an interview is underway although in an informal setting, and there is a general focus to the conversation. However, the researcher provides a minimum of direction to the discussion, thereby allowing many things to be brought up at any time during the interview. The informant is encouraged to speak in great depth on the topics, and the direction of the interview results from the responses of the informant, rather than a set of questions. This type of interviewing is often used to further refine the research domains, to identify appropriate language used by the population to describe the domains under study, and to describe in detail the context of the issue being researched. Information obtained from unstructured interviews is often used to construct interview guides for semi-structured interviews or focus groups.

Semi-structured interviews, another qualitative research method, (or "intensive interviews" [Berkowitz, 1996b]) are like unstructured interviews in that the setting may be informal and the informant is encouraged to speak in depth on specific topics. However, the interviewer uses a written interview guide with specific questions and generally has written instructions for how and when to probe for additional information. The interview guide is developed from the data obtained through informal and unstructured interviews. The interviewer provides more direction to the interview, and will try to obtain responses to each question on the interview guide. However, the number of questions is limited since the goal is to obtain in-depth information. This interview format is useful when follow-up in-depth interviews are not possible or to ensure consistency in data collection when there is more than one person conducting the interviews.

Structured interviews, (e.g., standardized questionnaires), a quantitative research method, are probably the most widely used data collection method for needs assessments. Structured interviews involve asking every person the same set of questions, most often in a questionnaire format with questions being asked in a specific order. In anthropology, structured interviews also include methods for systematically collecting information that can be compared across individuals, such as pile sorts, triad sorting (or triadic comparisons), rank ordering items and free listing, among others (Bernard, 1994; Weller and Romney, 1988). This chapter will only focus on the use of questionnaires as a structured interview.

Structured interviews using a questionnaire have several advantages, along with some disadvantages; advantages include ease of administration, ability to collect large amounts of information in a relatively short period of time, and ability to aggregate and analyze the data using statistical procedures. Reliability and validity may be at issue since survey instruments are infrequently evaluated on these two key elements. There may also be challenges in constructing the questionnaire to elicit community needs, rather than a community "wish list," and expectations that the survey will provide information for which it is not suitable (Bernard, 1994; Reviere et al., 1996; Witkin and Altschuld, 1995).

Witkin and Altschuld (1995) identify the following seven elements as essential elements to answer when planning the survey, once it is determined that a questionnaire is an appropriate method for data collection: target population, sampling, questionnaire administration, questionnaire design, item content, item formats and scales, and data analysis. The target population will be a key factor, first, to determine whether a survey is an appropriate method and second, to determine how it will be administered. A survey instrument can be administered as a mail survey, or telephone or one-on-one interviews. Each administration method has strengths and weaknesses, and the needs assessment team will have to decide which method is best considering the assessment scope, time frame, and budget. Mail surveys allow people to participate anonymously or, at minimum, maintain their confidentiality, are generally less expensive than in-person interviews (telephone or one-on-one) and can be distributed to a larger number of people. However, response rates can be very low leading to questions regarding generalizability of the data. In addition, individuals who respond to mailed surveys may be different from the population the needs assessment would like to reach, again leaving the question of validity of the information collected. And finally, mailed surveys must be very clear so that the respondent will easily understand what the question means. In a telephone or one-on-one interview, questions can be more complex since the interviewer takes the respondent through the interview and may be able to clarify, within the structured guidelines of the survey, questions that are not clear.

The second survey administration method is through telephone interviews. Telephone interviews offer similar levels of anonymity or confidentiality, are less expensive than one-on-one interviews and can provide a personal interaction similar to one-on-one interviews. The personal quality of the telephone interview may allow for a longer interview than a self-administered questionnaire would, although its length will, in general, be less than that of the one-on-one interview. Additionally, the higher quality of data generally obtained through telephone interviews may offset the increased cost over a mail survey (Berkowitz, 1996a). This method may not be appropriate if telephone service is limited in the target area or the target population has less access to telephone service than other population groups. In some urban areas, however, this may be the most effective way of reaching the male or female head of household.

In general, one-on-one interviews can be longer than a self-administered questionnaire or a telephone interview as a result of the interpersonal connection the interviewer creates with the respondent. The interviewer can also respond to questions about the study and clarify questions, within the guidelines of the structured interview format. One-on-one interviews may also allow the interviewer to access individuals in settings that might be more appropriate depending upon the survey topic, such as place of employment, social settings (e.g., parks, churches), and schools. Disadvantages include a relatively high cost in terms of time and money; lack of anonymity for the respondent, particularly when the topic is sensitive; and, in some areas, safety issues. In areas where the vast majority of the target population has a telephone, telephone administration of the survey instrument may be more cost-effective than one-on-one interviews. However, a good understanding of how the target population responds to survey research and the sensitivity of the questions on the questionnaire will determine whether a telephone or one-on-one interview should be undertaken.

Group Interviews. Group interviews are in-person interviews with several individuals. The most common type of group interview is the focus group. The second type of group interview, generally called group discussions, includes community forums, town hall meetings or other meetings where information is obtained from a group of people. Other group processess such as nominal group technique or the Delphi techniques are also types of group interviews (Berkowitz, 1996b; Bernard, 1994). This chapter, however, reviews only focus groups and group interviews because of the frequency with which they are used in needs assessments. Both focus groups and group discussions are also qualitative research methods.

Focus groups can be held at various points during the needs assessment. During the pre-assessment stage, a focus group can be held with the needs assessment team members to discuss openly and constructively issues and problems of relevance to the study. Focus groups can also be held with the stakeholders to ensure that the objectives and focus of the needs assessment are appropriate and well-targeted, and with members of the target population to gain additional insights to the data being collected.

Focus groups are in-person group interviews designed to identify and explore views on a given subject in an individual's own terms and framework of understanding; however, the question or questions are posed to a group for discussion. According to Krueger (1988: 18), a focus group is a "carefully planned discussion designed to obtain perceptions on a defined area of interest in a permissive, non-threatening environment" where "group members influence each other by responding to ideas and comments in the discussion." Focus group facilitation requires a high level of skill due to its highly structured format since the facilitator intentionally uses the group interaction to generate data. A typical focus group will have between 8 and 12 participants. Fewer than 5 participants results in limited diversity of opinion, while more than 12 may result in participants' inability to participate fully and a loss of interest in the process. Focus group participants are carefully selected according to characteristics relevant to the research question, e.g., live in the same geographic area, have similar occupations, be the same sex or age group, be of similar socio-economic status.

A focus group interview guide can be developed using data collected through unstructured individual interviews; the focus group, for example, can be used to investigate further how widespread certain beliefs are, whether specific behaviors are common, or how the community reacts to an intervention idea. Because participants can and will be influenced by other group participants, the researcher can analyze when and how shifts in opinion take place during the discussion, and identify factors that influenced the shift. For example, if the issue is a neighborhood beautification project and you wish to understand better why residents accept the accumulation of trash items in public areas, a focus group discussion could allow the researcher to examine how responsibility for public areas is determined individually and collectively, and how perceptions of responsibility might be influenced and modified. This information may then be used in a campaign to encourage individual participation in maintaining public areas in neighborhoods.

Advantages of a focus group include the ability to capture the dynamics of the group's interactions, greater candor on the part of participants when others admit to similar behaviors or attitudes, relatively low cost, the ability to include more individuals than individual interviews would allow, and fairly quick generation of data from multiple perspectives. Disadvantages include less facilitator control of the direction and pace of the group interview since the group's dynamics will influence this; challenges organizing the group, including identifying a convenient time and location for 8 to 12 people; the identification of appropriate participants; the need for highly skilled facilitators; and more complex data analysis since opinions may change over the course of the discussion, and those changes must be interpreted within the context of the group's interactions.

Group discussions offer an opportunity to collect useful information on a particular topic, without the highly structured format of a focus group. Unfortunately, due to the current popularity of "focus groups" as a means to collect information on any number of topics, many group discussions are classified as focus groups when, in reality, they were not (Krueger, 1988). This does not mean that information obtained from group discussions is not useful or valid; rather, it is just a different type of data. Group discussions can take place with a small number of people (e.g., a small group of neighbors) or in a large setting such as at a community forum. The facilitator may present the topic of interest and ask individuals to respond. In this format, there may be little interaction among the participants; rather, the interaction is between the facilitator and the individual, not the group. The group can therefore be very diverse, with limited sharing of personal information. Advantages include being able to use information collected from spontaneous group discussions or community forums called to discuss topics of relevance to the research question (e.g., trash collection services in the neighborhood).

A frequent question therefore, is when should individual interviews versus focus groups be used? Again, this will depend upon the type of information desired, the target population, as well as time and available funding.

Data Analysis

Scrimshaw and Hurtado (1987: 23) describe data analysis as "... not something to be done after all data have been collected, but rather [as] part of a continual process of examining the information as it comes in, classifying it, formulating additional questions, verifying the information, and developing conclusions." Bernard (1994: 360) describes data analysis as "... the search for patterns in data and ideas that help explain the existence of those patterns." A number of books exist that provide detailed descriptions on how to analyze qualitative and quantitative data (among others: Bernard, 1994; Krueger, 1988; Pelto and Pelto, 1987; Scrimshaw and Hurtado, 1987; Spradley, 1979; Weller and Romney, 1988; and numerous books on statistics). The analysis of any type of data takes skill and experience in order to take full advantage of the richness of the data, regardless of whether the data are qualitative or quantitative.

There are a number of methods to analyze qualitative data, and the analytic procedure will depend upon the needs assessment focus and the types of information collected. For unstructured, semi-structured, focus group and group discussion interviews the data are generally coded according to themes, words, meanings, images or other categories identified as relevant to the needs assessment (Grbich, 1999). Coding each time the theme or word or meaning is mentioned allows the researcher to compare how different informants categorize or describe the theme, as well as count how many times the theme or word or meaning is mentioned. This analysis of content may result in a taxonomy (a classification system) of a word or an event, leading to a profound understanding of local conceptual frameworks for that word or event. Coding may also provide sufficient numeric data for some quantitative analytic procedures, such as descriptive frequencies or simple bivariate analyses, to be conducted. Qualitative data can also be mapped in a flow chart (e.g., steps needed to access a specific service), as a cognitive map, or as a causal map (Bernard, 1994; Scrimshaw and Hurtado, 1987).

Quantitative data can be used to examine causal relationships through a number of statistical methods, starting with descriptive frequencies through factor analysis and regression models. The point is that the statistical tests used will depend upon the type of data and what the questions are.

FRAMING THE ISSUE

A needs assessment is a good way to examine how advocacy issues can be framed so that they resonate with the population the advocacy efforts are targeting. There may be multiple target populations, and these groups may be significantly different along a number of indicators. Therefore, it is essential to assess how the "need" can be presented in an appropriate manner. The results of a needs assessment may be used for a number of activities. For example, some data may support changes in the way a service is delivered (e.g., extended hours for immunization services to allow working parents greater flexibility), some data may support a more detailed community planning process for a specific activity (e.g., creation of a park as part of the neighborhood beautification project), and some data may be used to support advocacy efforts to raise awareness of something (e.g., the need for increased local or state funding for treatment and recovery programs). In work conducted by the Alliance Healthcare Foundation in San Diego, California, two key target populations were identified for the syringe exchange advocacy efforts carried out between 1994 and 1997: politicians and the general public (see case study below). It was hypothesized that the general public would be concerned primarily about disease transmission and risk to themselves and their families, with some interest about the cost of the disease to the public generally borne through health insurance premiums and public benefit programs. Politicians, on the other hand, would primarily be motivated by the cost to the public, which could result in funding shortfalls or rapidly increasing public expenditures on health care for severely ill and destitute residents. In order to frame the discussion for politicians, cost analyses with the estimated cost of current infections compared to the hypothetical number of infections that would have been averted had the intervention been in place were conducted as part of the needs assessment.

CASE STUDY

In 1993, the Alliance Healthcare Foundation (AHF) undertook a comprehensive needs assessment of injecting drug users in San Diego County (Alliance Healthcare Foundation, 1994). The AHF established a study group, composed of individuals with direct experience working with the target population and/or expertise in HIV/AIDS and substance abuse, to provide direction to the design and implementation of the needs assessment. The needs assessment included five components: a review of the scientific literature and epidemiological data on HIV/AIDS and hepatitis B, a survey of health and social service agencies in San Diego County, semi-structured interviews with injection drug users (IDUs) both in and out of treatment, a medical records review of HIV-positive and IDU-identified inmates in County detention facilities to assess health needs and cost to the public sector, and an estimation of the costs of HIV infection among IDUs with and without a syringe exchange program. The objectives of the needs assessment for San Diego's IDUs were the following:

1. To assess the culture and patterns of injection drug use, including ethnicity and geographic distribution;
2. To identify groups not traditionally associated with injection behaviors, e.g., vitamin, steroid and hormone injectors;
3. To estimate, using data collected from public and private organizations and agencies, and anecdotal data from outreach workers, the size and geographic spread of the IDU population of San Diego County; and

4. To provide recommendations for the Injection Drug Use Study Group on appropriate prevention strategies for HIV and other blood-borne diseases, and service needs of the IDU population.

Primary data collection was an important part of the needs assessment since data on utilization of general health and social services by IDUs were not available, and there was limited information available on reported needs of IDUs. The primary data collection consisted of a survey of organizations and agencies providing services specifically for IDUs or services that were needed by IDUs. Semi-structured open interviews were also conducted with IDUs who were not in treatment, IDUs using San Diego's underground needle exchange program, and IDUs in treatment. These interviews provided detailed information on injection equipment sharing, experiences with treatment programs, attitudes toward or use of a needle exchange program, and condom use. Consumer evaluation data on specific treatment programs was gathered from IDUs in treatment. The estimation of medical costs borne through public benefits programs was considered to be key for expanding the discussion of the impact of HIV/AIDS and hepatitis to the general public. Information was obtained by abstracting the medical records of 300 IDUs and 100 separate HIV-positive cases in San Diego County's detention facilities. Archival data from these records, in addition to supporting the well-documented connection between illicit drug use and incarceration, were used to estimate the cost of publicly funded treatment of inmates with HIV/AIDS and other medical conditions resulting from injection drug use. In addition, estimated cost impacts of HIV infection with and without a syringe exchange program were calculated using, in large part, the model developed for a similar analysis for the State of Hawaii in 1989.

Needs Assessment Methods

Literature Review

An extensive literature review on substance abuse and injection drug use, the cultures and behaviors of IDUs, and treatment models, especially clean syringe exchange and its effectiveness, was conducted.

Epidemiological Data

Epidemiological data on AIDS at the local (San Diego County), state (California) and national levels were collected. Data of relevance to injection drug use were also reviewed, including hepatitis B incidence and prevalence, and drug use patterns in San Diego as compared to the rest of the nation (from the Drug Use Forecasting System collected by the Department of Justice).

Agency Survey

A questionnaire was developed for a mail survey of organizations that either provided services specifically for IDUs or provided other services that IDUs may use. Information was collected on the general services provided by the organization, general client profile (including ethnicity, age, sex, sexual orientation, socioeconomic status and geographic locations), specific services provided to IDUs, client profile of their IDU population (the above-mentioned demographic information as well as estimated years of drug abuse), numbers of IDUs seen in treatment as well as outside of treatment programs, substances being injected, services being accessed by the IDU population, additional services needed for the population and estimated HIV seroprevalence of the IDU population. Surveys were mailed to local health agencies, hospitals, community clinics, community-based organizations, religious organizations, jails, probation departments, and drug treatment and rehabilitation centers, among others. A significant effort was made to include organizations not traditionally associated with service provision to IDUs or HIV-positive individuals. A 71% response rate was achieved through extensive, and time consuming, follow-up with each agency by telephone and through reminder letters.

Semi-Structured Open Interviews

Recognizing the diversity of the injecting drug using population in San Diego, study group members identified key subgroups for interviews. Semi-structured open interviews were carried out with five subgroups of injecting drug users: IDUs not in treatment, IDUs using the underground syringe exchange program (SEP) in San Diego, transgender IDUs not in treatment, IDUs in treatment programs, and gay male IDUs in a treatment program. A series of four interview guides, each specific to the group being targeted, was developed and reviewed by study group members and by outreach workers carrying out street outreach activities for HIV/AIDS prevention education and volunteers with the San Diego SEP. All interview guides were in English and in Spanish.

Outreach workers and SEP volunteers were identified as being the most appropriate individuals to conduct the interviews because of the existing relationships many had developed with their IDU clients. The interviewers reflected the diversity of the injecting drug users, with backgrounds and experience that included both men and women, Caucasian, African American and Latino individuals, all sexual orientations, and residence throughout the County. A characteristic that all the interviewers had in common was a deep personal interest in addressing the needs of the injecting drug using population. Interviewers were trained to obtain oral informed consent from the interview respondents. Both interviewers and respondents received a small stipend for their time, the receipt of which was not dependent upon whether the respondent completed the interview or not.

Medical Records Survey

With the historical and well-documented connection between illicit drug use and incarceration, study group members determined that data on local patterns of drug use would be important for identifying appropriate prevention and treatment modalities. Although the Drug Use Forecasting (DUF) reports produced by the Department of Justice capture some of this information, it was decided that the DUF data are somewhat limited and focus on developing strategies for drug control and enforcement. The information from the Sheriff's Medical Services offered the opportunity to examine injection drug use patterns in a larger context, encompassing health and treatment issues and, to some extent, the prevalence of HIV/AIDS in the jail system, particularly as it relates to injection drug use.

Medical records of 407 inmates (273 IDUs, 66 HIV-positive inmates, and 34 HIV-positive IDUs) admitted to the San Diego County Sheriff's Department Detention Facilities in a 12-month period were reviewed. Approximately 28 data elements, including demographics, drug use and treatment information, were collected from the IDU-identified case records; 19 data elements were collected from the HIV/AIDS-identified case records, and an additional 25 data elements were collected from the HIV/AIDS-identified cases records which were also IDU-identified. In addition, the Chief of Medical Records provided an estimate of the approximate costs of treating this population during their incarceration.

Cost Impact of HIV Infection in San Diego

In order to realistically begin discussion of a syringe exchange program as a harm reduction strategy in San Diego County, the economic costs and public health impact of high-risk injection behaviors among IDUs in the context of the HIV/AIDS epidemic were estimated. Estimates were calculated for three scenarios: (1) no access to an SEP, (2) limited access to the existing underground SEP, or (3) access to a legal SEP. The analyses were based, in part, upon a model used by the State of Hawaii prior to legislation authorizing the first legal SEPs in this state. The estimates for the total number of IDUs in the County, the number already seropositive, the seroconversion rate, the proportion already practicing safer injection behaviors, the proportion of IDUs that will practice safer injection behaviors after using the SEP, and the total lifetime cost for treating one case of AIDS were obtained using the limited data available. Information from the agency survey and the semi-structured open interviews was used to support the estimates.

Summary

Not all needs assessments need to be or should be as extensive as the one described. The type of needs assessment will depend upon the amount of information already available, the types of data available, the quality and reliability of the data, the priority or urgency of the issue to be investigated, and the level of funding available for the needs assessment. The Alliance Healthcare Foundation and the Study Group determined that the continuing transmission of HIV and hepatitis among injecting drug users and the lack of services for this marginalized population was a high priority for prevention and treatment efforts. However, there were little reliable data on the needs of IDUs in San Diego, the effectiveness of services designed to help IDUs and their sexual and needle-sharing partners reduce their risk of infectious diseases and on the effectiveness of different program modalities. The AHF used the needs assessment to focus its grantmaking efforts targeting substance abuse and communicable disease control and to develop a public education and advocacy campaign to educate elected officials and the general public on the benefits of comprehensive harm reduction strategies that include syringe exchange.

DISCUSSION QUESTIONS

1. You have been asked to conduct a needs assessment of Somali immigrants and refugees living in a large county in southern California. Develop a research question(s) and describe the methods you would use to conduct the needs assessment. Explain why each method was selected and its strengths and weaknesses.
2. You have just finished conducting a mental health needs assessment, and are very concerned with some of the findings regarding depression among youth in high school. Describe how you would use the results of the needs assessment and why you selected each activity.

REFERENCES

Alliance Healthcare Foundation (1994). *Injection Drug Use in San Diego County: A Needs Assessment. October 1994.* (pp. 1–237). San Diego, CA: Alliance Healthcare Foundation, website: www.alliancehf.org.

Berkowitz, S. (1996a). Creating the research design for a needs assessment. In R. Reviere, S. Berkowitz, C.C. Carter, C.G. Ferguson (Eds.), *Needs Assessment: A Creative and Practical Guide for Social Scientists* (pp. 15–31). Washington, D.C.:Taylor and Francis.

Berkowitz, S. (1996b). Using Qualitative and Mixed-Method Approaches. In R. Reviere, S. Berkowitz, C.C. Carter, C.G. Ferguson (Eds.), *Needs assessment: A Creative and Practical Guide for Social Scientists* (pp. 15–31). Washington, D.C.: Taylor and Francis.

Bernard, H.R. (1994). *Research Methods in Anthropology, Qualitative and Quantitative Approaches.* Thousand Oaks, CA: Sage Publications.

Burns, B. (1998). *Shelter: One Man's Journey from Homelessness to Hope.* Tucson, Arizona: University of Arizona Press.

Elliot, N.L., Quinless, F.W., & Parietti, E.S. (2000). Assessment of a Newark neighborhood: Process and outcomes. *Journal of Community Health Nursing, 17,* 211–224.

Grbich, C. (1999). *Qualitative Research in Health: An Introduction.* Thousand Oaks, CA: Sage Publications.

Kaufman, R. (2000). *Mega Planning: Practical Tools for Organizational Success.* Thousand Oaks, CA: Sage Publications.

Krueger, R.A. (1988). *Focus Groups: A Practical Guide for Applied Research.* Newbury Park, California: Sage Publications.

Lasker, R.D. and the Committee on Medicine and Public Health (1997). *Medicine and Public Health, the Power of Collaboration.* New York: The New York Academy of Medicine.

National Council of La Raza, (1995). *Using Data, Assessing Needs: A Guide for Community Members of HIV Prevention Community Planning Groups.* Washington, D.C.: NCLR.

Pelto, P.J., Pelto, G.H. (1987). *Anthropological Research: The Structure of Inquiry,* 2nd ed. Cambridge: Cambridge University Press.

Reviere, R., Berkowitz, S., Carter, C.C., Ferguson, C.G. (1996). Introduction: Setting the stage. In R. Reviere, S. Berkowitz, C.C. Carter, C.G. Ferguson (Eds.), *Needs Assessment: A Creative and Practical Guide for Social Scientists* (pp. 1–12). Washington, D.C.: Taylor and Francis.

Scrimshaw, S.C.M., Hurtado, E. (1987). *Rapid Assessment Procedures for Nutrition and Primary Health Care.* Los Angeles: UCLA Latin American Center Publications, University of California, Los Angeles.

Spradley, J.P. (1988). *The Ethnographic Interview.* Fort Worth, Texas: Holt, Rinehart, and Winston, Inc.

Weller, S.C., & Romney, A.K. (1988). *Systematic Data Collection.* Newbury Park, CA: Sage Publications.

Witkin, B.R., & Altschuld, J.W. (1995). *Planning and Conducting Needs Assessments: A Practical Guide.* Thousand Oaks, CA: Sage Publications.

CHAPTER THREE

Organizing Community
Grassroots Activism

Every moment is an organizing opportunity, every person a potential activist, every
minute a chance to change the world.
Dolores Huerta

This chapter focuses on a brief description of basic concepts and definitions,
theoretical models, and strategies for community organizing, as described
in the literature. This is followed by examples of successful organizations
that began as grassroots efforts at change.

BASIC CONCEPTS AND DEFINITIONS

Community Organizing

Community organizing is defined simply by Labonte (1994: 261) as
"the process of organizing people around problems or issues that are larger
than group members' own immediate concerns." Minkler's (1978: 198) definition encompasses "efforts by which groups sharing a common interest
are assisted in identifying their specific needs and goals, mobilizing resources within their communities, and in other ways taking action leading
to the achievement of the goals they have set collectively." These activities build and enhance the power of community members through activism and involvement (Mosher, 1999). Central to modern community
organizing is representation and participation, engaging the community
organizer, expert professionals, and the community/group constituency.

A wide variety of forms exist, ranging from "bottom-up" to "top-down," with "citizen control" or "organizer manipulation." (Rosenau, 1994).

Grassroots Approaches

Grassroots approaches are "bottom-up" strategies with the design and implementation of program or policy goals and guidelines driven by community members themselves (Treno and Holder, 1997a). According to Mosher (1999), grassroots approaches serve as the foundation for policy change. Minkler (1978) considers the active involvement of people at the grassroots or community level to be the only true form of community organizing, with community members themselves identifying and defining their needs and goals. The opposite "top-down" approach is driven by experts outside of the community or by self-identified community leaders (Treno and Holder, 1997a). Under this approach, the community or client group may not play a major role in the formulation of social planning and health functions (Mosher, 1999). Underlying the grassroots approach is the belief that programs or strategies are more effective if the effort originates with community members, local organizations and local leaders, and includes a wide spectrum of community members in the efforts. Inclusion increases a sense of ownership that can provide a feeling of powerfulness. (Treno and Holder, 1997a).

There is nothing inherent in a grassroots approach that automatically ensures program success. A grassroots approach may be limited due to a lack of local experience or expertise to effectively design and implement strategies (Treno and Holder, 1997a). Ideally, outside community organizers, public health professionals or other experts can be utilized to address these shortcomings and to play a vital role in supporting grassroots efforts, but they must be careful to limit that role to consultant or technical advisor. This entails carefully listening to and documenting concerns voiced by the community. Outsiders' service in leadership roles or their formulation of the agenda negates the central premise and goal for grassroots organizing (Mosher, 1999).

Empowerment

Empowerment is central to the concept and practice of community organizing and is a requirement for the genuine representation and participation of communities. Rosenau (1994) defines empowerment in the modern sense as the acquisition of information, skills, and resources to enable and enhance decision-making power by individuals or groups. People who wish to exercise power must be organized. According to Minkler (1992), "If power is the ability to predict, control and participate in one's environment, then empowerment is the process by which individuals and communities are enabled to take such power and act effectively in changing their lives and their environment" (Minkler, 1992: 303). Merideth (1994: 360) further defines empowerment as "fundamentally a process of collective reflection and action in which previously isolated individuals become protagonists in shaping society according to their shared interests."

In community organizing, empowerment occurs simultaneously on two levels: individual and community. For an individual, increased social support and a sense of control and self-determination may enhance confidence, ability to cope, and satisfaction with life. Community-level empowerment results in increased community competence, the ability to collaborate effectively to identify problems, set goals, and take action through collective problem-solving (Minkler, 1992). This may enable "people to begin to transform situations of oppression into opportunities for critical reflection, dialogue and liberation" (Merideth, 1994: 367). Flick, Reese, Rogers, Fletcher and Sonn (1994) conclude that community empowerment implies significant community control, with voting privileges and position of power limited to the community constituency and the role of outside advisors and experts extremely limited.

Three guiding principles for community organizing in relation to community empowerment are described by Speer and Hughey (1995) in the work of the Pacific Institute for Community Organizations (PICO), a community organizing network with organizations in 25 cities across the United States. These are: (1) empowerment can only be realized through organization, (2) social power is built on the strength of interpersonal relationships, and (3) individual empowerment must be grounded in a dialectic of action and reflection.

Advocacy and the Role of Public Health

Labonte (1994: 263) defines advocacy as "taking a position on an issue, and initiating actions in a deliberate attempt to influence private and public policy choices." Outside institutions, public health professionals, or other experts can play a vital role in supporting successful advocacy efforts. Health organizations and institutions, acknowledged for their powerful role in defining what is important in social life and political discourse, can assist in the creation of policy documents and analyses, "thereby legitimizing the advocacy concerns of community groups with which they work," and "the policies they create and make public" (Labonte, 1994: 263). Individually or through their professional organizations, professionals can voice their collective concerns on matters of social policy, such as social welfare reforms, housing needs or affordability, employment policies, and environmental standards.

THEORETICAL MODELS OF COMMUNITY ORGANIZING

Four theoretical models of community organizing are described: social movement, Paolo Freire's education for critical consciousness, Saul Alinsky's community organization theory, and post-modern theory. These models are not discrete approaches, but clearly overlap, and in practice are used in combination.

Social Movement

Hatfield's (1991) research suggests that a social movement arises spontaneously when a group of people give up on finding solutions to a problem individually and begin to take collective action to solve the common problem. First, the dissatisfaction must be recognized by individuals and shared with others. Second, the group needs to: (1) believe in its ability to resolve the issue as a group, rather than individuals; (2) live in a situation that facilitates the members' ability to come together effectively; and (3) feel strongly enough about making a change to risk opposition for changing existing traditions and beliefs. The group of discontented individuals then develops goals and strategies, and works toward social change to address the underlying problem.

Education For Critical Consciousness (Freire)

Action based on critical reflection is the central theme of this theory. According to Merideth (1994), the educational philosophy and methodology advocated by Paolo Freire suggests that the well-being of both the community and the individual must be understood in terms of respective social, political, and economic challenges. Community organizers must go beyond merely educating and engage themselves with the daily struggles of their client, acting as catalysts to create "critical consciousness among community members" and to promote "collective action to address the political and economic forces that affect health" (Merideth, 1994: 357).

The community organizer's goal is to promote self-reliance for both individual and group empowerment, based on lessons learned from people's own life experiences. The relationship between educators and learners must be equitable and mutually respectful. Education for critical consciousness is thereby used as an approach to individual and social transformation or action for social change. This process is ongoing with continual reflection and self-critique as part of daily activities personally and in the broader social context (Merideth, 1994). "Liberating dialogue" is espoused by Freire to critically examine the world and take action to change it, with "teacher-learners" using problem-solving techniques to facilitate discussion, and "learner-teachers" working with them in small groups or "culture circles." Wallerstein and Bernstein's three-stage summary of empowerment education simplifies these concepts to include listening to understand key themes or issues of the community; participatory dialogue around these key issues; and action as a result of the process (Minkler, 1992).

Community Organization Theory (Alinsky)

Minkler (1992) describes the model proposed by Saul Alinsky as a set of principles and approaches for effectuating change, rather than a coherent theory. This approach is based on a perception of the low-income community as relatively powerless and disenfranchised. The aim is to facilitate a process for people with a shared interest or concern to identify a target, marshal resources, and mobilize action with the ultimate goal of realigning power within the community. To be effective, community organizing must develop local leadership to increase the problem-solving capacity of the community. Meredith (1994) suggests that the process of transforming problems into successes on specific issues serves to broaden the base of support and give people a sense of their own power. The organizer needs to give the people the feeling that they can do something, and then reinforce this by actually achieving the work.

Alinsky's organizing model is careful to limit the role and functions of the outside organizer to that of a change catalyst in fostering local leadership and capacity building. The organizer is there at the invitation of the community and must remain in the background while accomplishing these objectives. Through individual and collective empowerment and transformation for change, the organizer uses the experiences of people to begin an educational process that encourages them to problematize the issues they are facing in reflecting on their lives, and to seek solutions and change. "Starting where people are does not mean staying there"

(Merideth, 1994: 365). Once internal leadership is in place and continuity is ensured, the organizer withdraws (Minkler, 1985; Merideth, 1994).

Post-Modern Theory

Rosenau (1994) concludes that health politics and community health organizing will be even more challenging in a post-modern society, with responsibility and traditional forms of community of diminished significance. In contrast to the "modern" community organizing tradition that emerged in the 1950s and 1960s and has been described prior to this section, post-modern theory questions conventional community organizing concepts in community health promotion. Post-modernists posit that an individual can, in reality, represent only him- or herself, thereby calling into question the modern concept of representation and participation. This perspective has been espoused by AIDS activists and patients, who defend their "right to self-representation," particularly in regard to their own health care. Post-modernists may consequently be skeptical of government programs that require the participation of individuals that fit specific demographic or organizational profiles to provide respective community representation in health planning. The value of empowerment, a cornerstone of modern grassroots organizing, is also called into question by post-modernists. Post-modernists tend to embrace the concept of empowerment only as it relates to an individual in enhancing his/her self-development or self-preoccupation. Post-modern social movements are characterized by their tolerance, political pluralism, grassroots activities, and the formation of temporary coalitions to achieve issue-specific aims. ACT UP, a clear example of a social movement influenced by this post-modern perspective, is described later in this chapter.

Post-modern theory posits that grassroots "bottom-up" initiatives from within the community, rather than programs deemed to be beneficial for a particular population by an outside expert or professional, will be the most effective approaches in the future. Post-modern community organizing requires that organizers (1) take people seriously, listen, wait and be patient; (2) show respect for individual preferences, even when they are contradictory, ill-informed, self-destructive, and lacking coherence; (3) accept that you cannot do for people what they must do for themselves, when and if they are ready; (4) be realistic; don't expect changes in the short term; (5) emphasize choices rather than use a take-it-or-leave-it approach; (6) don't discount the irrational, emotional and intuitive; they are a significant and driving source of human existence; (7) do not expect consistency;

"a thousand points of light" may mean speaking with a thousand different voices (Rosenau, 1994).

COMMUNITY MOBILIZATION

Community organizing is used to mobilize communities for institutional and policy change (Wagenaar, Murray, Gehan, Wolfson, Forster, Toomey, Perry, and Jones-Webb, 2000). Community participation and involvement are not ends in themselves, but rather are a means by which to instigate social action and/or achieve democratic control with regard to program decisionmaking (Merideth, 1994). According to Treno and Holder (1997b), community mobilization includes all activities that prepare the community to accept and support a concept or strategy prior to taking action. It is an outgrowth and part of community organizing and creating community concerns about an issue.

As with other concepts of community organizing, Treno and Holder (1997a) posit that successful community mobilization must be grassroots-based and reflective of community-identified needs. They suggest that three factors are essential to successful community mobilization through a grassroots approach: (1) the multi-sectoral inclusion (involvement) of community in all aspects of the program; (2) the development of organizational linkages characterized by inter-group and cross-sector communication, coordination and collaboration; and (3) adequate access to and control of resources to support community policy-related decisionmaking.

Understanding and assessment of the community's "readiness" is a crucial factor in organizing for mobilization. Communities with a stronger sense of identity, cohesiveness and interconnectedness are more likely to be able to mobilize to solve their own problems (Flick et al., 1994). Communities that successfully organized in response to AIDS, for example, typically had some historic cohesiveness in mobilizing around other health and social concerns (Martin, Galvan, Perini, Morgante, 1991). On the other hand, the greater the degree of social stratification and separation in the community, the less likely that community-wide participation in mobilizing efforts will occur (Ugalde, 1985). Groups with less power may attempt to rectify their situations by limiting the power other groups have over them (Labonte, 1994).

Labonte (1994) suggests that conflict is healthy and may be an important mechanism for mobilization; the use of a confrontational approach to organizing has historically been successful in creating and mobilizing community groups from states of isolation and complacency. By simultaneously nurturing consensual, caring social relations, both parties can benefit from the outcome, including those who enjoy greater privileges.

According to Moss (2000), the moral crusade serves as the basic strategy for the development of health initiatives. Most, if not all, of the successful grassroots movements in the United States today have as their basis a moral crusade of some type. While liberals traditionally associate moral crusades with conservatives, particularly in relation to drugs or sex, it is important to acknowledge that the movement to fund AIDS research and treatment in the United States was a moral crusade that was initiated and maintained by gay activism and a vision of a society in which understanding, rather than stigmatization, would prevail. The ultimate success of that movement as a moral crusade was a lesson that AIDS activists took to heart, together with subsidiary lessons on the importance of activism, the need to mobilize patients to further these goals, and the power of the media. These lessons were subsequently adopted by other disease constituencies, and now form an integral part of public health. The harm reduction/needle exchange movement, "a child of AIDS activism," is another example of a moral crusade, combining drugs, a large issue that has historically been framed in an opposing moral context, with AIDS.

Moral crusades can have drawbacks. Aiming at emotions rather than intellect may provoke guilt or fear. In the "age of spin," these emotional responses are easily amplified. Conducting public health by moral crusade may seriously limit the movement's direction, scope and adaptability to changing circumstances and information. Moral crusades deal in certainties, with any deviation from the central issue considered "heresy or sin." Once adopted as policy, this may negate the ability to accept or incorporate new research that does not support the central moral premise (Moss, 2000).

STRATEGIES FOR COMMUNITY ORGANIZING AND MOBILIZATION

Events as well as people are often spontaneous catalysts to organizing around an issue. The origins of Mothers Against Drunk Driving (MADD) and the Million Mom March began with events that spurred individuals to collectively begin to take action. In the case of ACT UP and the National Committee for Mental Hygiene, an impassioned plea for change by an individual was the motivating factor. Outsiders interested in organizing communities also need to successfully identify individuals or events as entry points to motivate change within a community.

Access, as defined by the ability of a community organizer to meet easily with the population members and the degree of ease with which members can meet with each other, is critical. Significant barriers or challenges to access may include geographic dispersion of the community, time constraints of members, finding a comfortable or safe meeting location, level of trust, legal intervention and repression, and fear of being seen or identified. The time and effort required to organize is directly correlated to community readiness, group identity and the degree of existing access of group members to each other. A willingness to meet people "where they are" helps to create an atmosphere of good faith by reducing the fear of manipulation and by increasing credibility. The best approach to gain support for organizing around an issue is to begin with an issue that entails only minor modifications in behavior or lifestyle and results in a significant and visible improvement, thereby creating a sense of accomplishment and identity for the group when that goal is attained. More drastic changes and concepts are less likely to initially gain group acceptance (Martin et al., 1991).

Indigenous Community Organizer

According to Treno and Holder (1997b), the first step in community organizing is the recruitment, hiring and training of local members of the community as program staff, whether paid or volunteer, beginning with the program coordinator for the entire project. This must be a respected and capable individual who can carry out the wide range of required activities. The coordinator should work with local interested group members and leaders to begin to establish the group or organization. The group or organization should ultimately assume responsibility for subsequent organizing activities, with the assistance of the organizer. Wagenaar and colleagues (2000) found that local community members inexperienced in community organizing could successfully be hired, trained and developed into community organizers.

The identification and recruitment of community leaders or opinion-leaders who influence and represent the larger constituency of the community is critical to successful community organizing. To ensure success and future sustainability, all proposed activities should be built into pre-existing social structures, communication lines and general group infrastructure by or with the assistance of identified community gatekeepers (Martin et al., 1991).

Contingent upon the degree of community readiness, Treno and Holder (1997b) suggest that a substantial period of time may be needed to develop the group and its leadership, and to develop specific strategies for action. The program coordinator needs to meet with the group to identify issues and to develop implementation strategies most relevant to their community. Additional targeted task forces may be developed as needed for different issues and/or strategies.

Small Group Development

Although the "community" is considered the nexus of empowerment and action, the small group is more accurately the "locus of change" where identities are forged and purpose is created. Interaction with others in a small group setting promotes the development of a sense of control and a feeling of connectedness and encourages critical thinking. Ultimately, small group development helps to create the skills and confidence necessary to participate in the more formalized action of advocacy. Without small group support, many individuals would remain marginalized and uninvolved (Labonte, 1994).

For marginalized individuals who do not self-identify as a "group" with any kind of shared purpose or traditions, the community-building process can be extremely slow. While outside program funders and staff may expect groups to move quickly into action once resources are provided, it may actually take several years for a group of initially disconnected and disenfranchised individuals to begin to self-identify as members of a "group," and much longer to develop the group dynamics, skills and sense of empowerment necessary to address larger issues of concern. Additionally, group tension and anxiety may arise with a shift toward an outward orientation from the interpersonal security developed within the group. Small group developers or community organizers must be extremely cognizant of the need to support empowerment simultaneously at both the internal (personal or interpersonal) and external (sociopolitical) levels in a complementary, not contradictory fashion (Labonte, 1994). Minkler (1978; 1985; 1992) successfully used this strategy to organize marginalized elderly poor in the Tenderloin Senior Organizing Project (TSOP) in San Francisco.

Town Hall Meeting

The town hall meeting or large community group meeting can be used as a forum to organize, inform and empower a community into action. Ideally, the meeting agenda allows participants to exchange information individually and collectively, identify issues and concerns on one or more topics of common interest, consider creative solutions, and suggest next steps and/or develop a plan of action. Community, government, and institutional leaders can also be invited to hear first-hand the opinions of members of their constituency, and to suggest solutions. Unlike the small group approach, the success of this strategy requires a higher degree of community readiness and problem-solving capacity, with some shared sense of identity around an issue that will attract participants in the first place. ACT UP, described later in this chapter, and the National Coalition for Cancer Survivorship (NCCS) have successfully used this strategy in organizing their constituencies.

The NCCS uses town hall meetings as a platform for people affected by cancer to express their views about this disease, both in community and national settings. Since its first town hall meeting in 1994, 30 or more town hall meetings have been held across the United States, with local organizing efforts primarily driven by cancer survivors, utilizing NCCS guidelines. Participants include not only cancer survivors and their families, but also healthcare professionals, local and state legislators, community leaders and the media. Participants have advocated for the recognition of cancer as the nation's healthcare priority, equal access to quality care, increased funding for research, and support for cancer advocacy efforts. Cancer survivors call on their peers to become informed, responsible and empowered advocates for their own care, ensuring that the healthcare professionals who are treating them hear and understand their issues and needs (Johnson, Blanchard and Harvey, 2000).

Marches and Rallies

Marches and rallies can offer the same impact as the town hall meeting as a point around which to organize or expand a grassroots organization. Marches and rallies are conducted on an even larger scale and encompass a greater geographic area of support. Based on the success of its town hall meetings, the NCCS sponsored the THE MARCH—Coming Together To Conquer Cancer, a national rally held in Washington, D.C. in September 1998 (Johnson, Blanchard and Harvey, 2000).

The Million Mom March (MMM), a national grassroots, chapter-based movement, was organized specifically around a national march. MMM is dedicated to the prevention of death and injury associated with gun use and the provision of support to victims and survivors of gun violence. MMM began in the summer of 1999 with a call to action by a horrified and frustrated New Jersey mother after watching the shootings at the Granada Hills Day Camp unfold on television. After nine months of planning and organizing, more than 750,000 mothers and "honorary moms" (fathers, uncles, friends, etc.) marched on the National Mall in Washington, D.C. on Mother's Day of 2000, while tens of thousands of others marched in towns scattered throughout the country. Demonstrating their support for reasonable gun laws to keep children safe, one MMM slogan clearly stated the issue: "It is easier to child-proof your gun than bullet-proof your child!" MMM subsequently merged with the Brady Campaign and the Brady Center to Prevent Gun Violence (Tanner, 2000; Million Mom March, 2002).

Ultimately, the success of an organization depends on more than raw emotion. MADD (2002) suggests the following elements as vital to any group establishing itself as a force for change: (1) a charismatic spokesperson; (2) a name that is catchy or symbolic; (3) a simple mission statement, (4) a financial and emotional mentor; (6) enthusiastic volunteers; (7) the support of national legislators; (8) compliance with all government and Better Business Bureau requirements; (9) visibility in the media; (10) a diverse leadership; and (11) diverse sources of funds.

THE CYCLE OF ORGANIZING AND MOBILIZATION

Speer and Hughey (1995), in their review of the PICO network, describe organizing as a cycle consisting of four interrelated phases: assessment, research, action and reflection. Following is a review of this cycle, incorporating concepts from two studies of community organizing suggested by Labonte (1994) and Mayster, Waitzkin, Hubbell and Rucker (1990). The latter is based in the community grassroots organizing and advocacy work of the Orange County Task Force on Indigent Health Care.

This cycle of organizing and mobilization implies that (1) organization is a prerequisite for community empowerment, (2) the strength of relationships between organizational members constitutes the foundation of the organization, and (3) relationships develop as a function of mutual action and reflection. Ultimately, all collective effort is carried out by individuals. (Speer and Hughey, 1995).

Assessment

Assessment is the process by which members identify and define the critical issues affecting their community. This information-gathering through informal face-to-face meetings facilitates dialogue and deepens interpersonal relationships among community members. Power grows through relationships, and issues identified through assessment focus the organization through the next three phases (Speer and Hughey, 1995).

In addition to its organizing significance, detailed activities entailed in this phase are discussed in Chapter 2.

Research

Research is the examination of causes and correlates of issues identified in the assessment phase: the nature of the issue, including any barriers to access and/or limitations of current policies and how the allocation of community resources relates to it; political influences, how organizations or other players exercise social power around it; and solutions. This information is used to raise consciousness about the issue and ultimately to buttress subsequent political strategies that target government and institutional policies. This phase is conducted through meetings with knowledgeable community members and experts or entities from inside or outside the organization. Labonte (1994) suggests that "legitimating professionals" within the organization can create a "strong inner arm" by providing the required research studies. Members of the Orange County Task Force on Indigent Health Care chose to prioritize studies that potentially could impact local policy relatively quickly (Mayster et al., 1990).

Action

Action is the exercise of the social power of the organization through public events that demonstrate that power. The action phase begins with strategy development. The strategy is based on information uncovered in the research phase, highlighting any contradictions between the expressed values and priorities of the community and actual practices, policies, or funding priorities. Despite variability in local conditions, advocacy gains strength when it is multifaceted and tailored to local needs, politics, and policies.

Labonte (1994) warns, however, that effective strategies to change policy must seek control of both political and related economic aspects to be effective. Policy is often set within narrow parameters without substantial control over economic resources, which can make them virtually meaningless. In developing such a strategy, activists can generally enhance their impact if they include components of short-term research, political work aiming to reduce barriers to access, and focused legal action based on cases whose resolution can lead to policy change.

Members are next mobilized to participate in collective action to present the research findings and the proposed mechanism to resolve the contradictions. This phase culminates in public meetings or events to bring together the organization's members and supporters with the media, public officials, and other concerned citizens and organizations. The organization's power is often directed toward a specific target, such as institutions, government or other policymakers in order to shift the allocation of community resources (Speer and Hughey, 1995). The collective action may be conducted in the political, legislative, regulatory, and/or judicial contexts and extend beyond the local level to regional, state, and national levels. Political strategies for policy change buttressed by research was the principle activity of the Orange County Task Force on Indigent Health Care (Mayster et al., 1990).

These efforts can be enhanced through the provision of personal stories by activist groups and impacted citizens outside of the organization (Labonte, 1994). Coalition building and advocacy, described in Chapter 4, often overcome the political limitations of community organizing.

Reflection

Reflection allows members to consider how the organization evolved through the organizing cycle. This entails an examination of the effectiveness of implemented strategies, the identification of emerging leadership, a consideration of how social power was demonstrated, and an examination of future directions for the organization. The process is cyclical, ending and then beginning again with a new assessment (Speer and Hughey, 1995). As the cycle successfully repeats itself, the organized entity achieves recognition and legitimacy.

GRASSROOTS ADVOCACY IN ACTION

Organized grassroots advocacy efforts occur frequently throughout the United States. Much of this work has received limited attention in the published literature. The reviews that have been conducted of grassroots organizations and movements indicate that these movements have developed distinct approaches and strategies in response to diverse health and social issues, to discrimination, to threats to personal safety, and to the concerns of disenfranchised or stigmatized communities. The foci of such movements have included the effects of drinking and driving (AIM, Alliance Against Intoxicated Motorists; BACCHUS, Boost Alcohol Consciousness Concerning the Health of University Students; MADD, Mothers Against Drunk Driving; RID, Remove Intoxicated Drivers; and SADD,

Students Against Driving Drunk); the prevention of death and injury from guns (the Million Mom March and the Brady Campaign) and of child abuse and neglect (the Family Life Development Center at Cornell University); indigent health care (Orange County Task Force On Indigent Health Care); the promotion of health and the development of leadership among Mexican immigrants (Casa en Casa) and among low-income seniors (TSOP, Tenderloin Senior Organizing Project); and the alleviation of discrimination and stigma associated with mental illness (NMHA, National Mental Health Association and NAMI, National Alliance for the Mentally Ill), with cancer (NCCS, National Coalition for Cancer Survivorship), and with AIDS (ACT UP) (Foulks, 2000; Johnson, Blanchard and Harvey, 2000; Tanner, 2000; Merideth, 1994; Arno and Feiden, 1992; Mayster et al., 1990; Ungerleider and Bloch, 1988; Minkler, 1985; Barry, 1982).

These groups have historically used multiple strategies simultaneously or sequentially to organize and empower their constituency to achieve their goals. These strategies include the creation of group identity and ownership around issues, community education, the use of mass media to enhance awareness, the provision of assistance in the development of curricula for colleges and secondary schools, and advocacy with legislators and policymakers to strengthen existing law and policy and to formulate new law and policy. Detailed descriptions of three successful grassroots movements follow: the National Mental Health Association (NMHA), the National Alliance for the Mentally Ill (NAMI) and ACT UP.

National Mental Health Association (NMHA)

The National Mental Health Association (NMHA) is the nation's only non-government citizens' voluntary organization focused on all aspects of mental illnesses and mental health, with more than 340 affiliates nationwide. The organization seeks to promote mental health and prevent mental disorders through advocacy, education, research and service (National Mental Health Association, 2002). Additionally, the NMHA seeks change in societal attitudes toward mental illnesses and the improvement of services for those with mental illness (Foulks, 2000).

The NMHA was formed in 1950 as the National Association for Mental Health (NAMH) following the merger of three organizations: the National Mental Health Foundation, the National Committee for Mental Hygiene and the Psychiatric Foundation. The organization formally changed its name to the National Mental Health Association in 1979.

NAMH's first precursor, the National Committee for Mental Hygiene, was founded in 1909 by Clifford Beers, a former mental health patient who reported on his horrifying treatment experience in his now famous book, *A Mind That Found Itself*. The attention created by Beers' book enabled him to form a coalition of powerful figures from psychology, psychiatry, finance and politics to address the treatment of mental illness. The goals of the National Committee for Mental Hygiene were: (1) to improve attitudes toward mental illness and the mentally ill; (2) to improve services for the mentally ill; and (3) to work for the prevention of mental illness and promote mental health.

The National Mental Health Foundation began in 1943 when a group of conscientious objectors, who had been put to work in mental hospitals and there experienced the shameful conditions of care for the mentally ill, were inspired to advocate for change. Subsequent attention by the media resulted in a 13-page article entitled 'Bedlam 1946, Most U.S. Mental Hospitals Are Ashamed and Disgraced,' published in the May 13, 1946 issue of *Life* magazine along with photographs of deplorable hospital conditions. In the same year, the novel, *The Snake Pit*, was published, which detailed the horrifying experiences of a woman confined in a psychiatric hospital. The book became a best-seller, and inspired a movie by the same name (Foulks, 2000). The third partner in the creation of NAMH, the Psychiatric Foundation, was an offshoot of the American Psychological Organization and was concerned primarily with fundraising (National Mental Health Association, 2002).

In the 1950s, the NAMH advocated nationally for a shift in treatment for mentally ill persons from the large state hospitals to community mental health centers. During the same time period, the first use of phenothiazine (a tranquilizer) in the United States also allowed many patients to leave the hospital. In 1953, the National Association for Mental Health collected the shackles used to chain mental patients in state hospitals and forged them into The Bell of Hope, which stands today as a symbol of the NMHA (former NAMH). By the mid-1950s, the NAMH had 40 divisions and 700 affiliated chapters. NAMH joined with the Congressionally-mandated Joint Commission on Mental Illness and Health to develop *Action for Mental Health*, a report published in 1960 which laid the foundation for further accelerated de-hospitalization. Between 1955 and 1994 the number of patients in state hospitals was reduced more than seven-fold. The NAMH expanded its mission to include the prevention of chronic mental illness, and incorporated the National Organization for Mentally Ill Children (Foulks, 2000).

NMHA's effectiveness is attributable to several factors. These include: (1) a nationwide presence with a network of affiliates providing a strategic local presence for advocacy and education efforts; (2) advocacy leadership with a strong voice at the federal, state and local levels for policies that expand opportunities for people with mental illness; (3) a broad-based perspective, representing a diverse network of mental health consumers, advocates, family members, providers and other stakeholders who work together to promote the importance of mental health in all aspects of health and in all stages of life; (4) coalitions and partnerships that bring together different factions to address complex issues; (5) a consumer focus on individuals with mental illnesses, with an emphasis on consumer participation and empowerment in all activities; (6) advocacy efforts on behalf of children; and (7) education and communications expertise, with a successful track record in developing strong media relationships and public education and communication strategies (National Mental Health Association, 2002).

NMHA's *National Public Education Campaign on Clinical Depression*, begun in 1993, informs Americans about symptoms of depression and provides information about treatment. NMHA advocates for parity of mental health benefits with other health coverage. Other NMHA programs include: (1) the Campaign for America's Mental Health, designed to increase the numbers of individuals who seek and receive treatment for mental illnesses and to improve the detection and treatment of mental disorders in primary care settings; (2) Partners in CARE, to promote and develop model community-based services for adults with schizophrenia and other serious mental illnesses; (3) the Children's Mental Health Matters Campaign, a comprehensive national grassroots initiative to increase understanding of children's mental health disorders among educators, primary care providers, and families; (4) justice programs to educate the public and policymakers about the large numbers of youth and adults in the justice system who have untreated mental and emotional disorders; and (5) the Safe Schools/Healthy Students Action Center, designed to provide ongoing technical assistance on a nationwide basis to school districts seeking preventive mental health services for students. Additional programs include the Mental Health Information Center, College Students and Depression, Children's Linkages, Childhood Depression Awareness Day, May is Mental Health Month, Stigma Watch and Mental Health Media Awards. NMHA's other activities include federal and state advocacy efforts to improve the country's treatment of people with mental illnesses and efforts to increase consumer support and to empower voters (National Mental Health Association, 2002).

National Alliance for the Mentally Ill (NAMI)

NAMI was organized by family members in response to trends in psychiatric practice and theory in the 1960s and 1970s, which blamed the onset of mental illness in individuals on the actions of their parents. This approach resulted in the stigmatization of both the patients and their families. Even though these theories were widely accepted by professionals, the theories could neither explain nor provide a cure for devastating mental illnesses (Foulks, 2000). The NAMI movement also stemmed from dissatisfaction with the lack of services and resources for the mentally ill, the overwhelming burden of caring for mentally ill patients that was placed on their families, and the callousness of the professionals who did serve this population. Acknowledgment of this shared pain and suffering began to bring parents together in support groups that evolved quickly into a social movement committed to change (Hatfield, 1991).

Beginning in 1977, the Community Support Program (CSP) of the National Institute of Mental Health (NIMH) attempted to formulate a comprehensive model of community care based on a rehabilitative treatment approach that would be sensitive to client needs. This effort was, in large part, an attempt to address problems resulting from the deinstitutionalization of clients from long-term institutions. The CSP turned to families of seriously mentally ill adults for support of these efforts. As opportunities increased for families across the country to meet through CSP meetings and Community Health Center boards, they began to compare notes on available treatments, approaches of professionals, and their experiences. They began to doubt the validity of the dominant psychiatric theories, the effectiveness of the prescribed remedies, and the resulting stigmatization (McLean, 2000). In 1979, Beverly Young and Harriet Shetler, each with a child with schizophrenia, decided to hold a national meeting of family members of mentally ill persons to develop resources to help families cope. In September 1979 in Madison, Wisconsin, they formed a new grassroots advocacy organization, the National Alliance for the Mentally Ill or AMI (later NAMI), meaning 'love' or 'friendship'. Common painful experiences of attendees created immediate empathy and solidarity (Foulks, 2000).

Many active NAMI members came from or were well connected politically and socially with licensed mental health and other professionals, academia, or high military posts, and were able to enlist and leverage support from these arenas. As a result, NAMI received support early on from NIMH leaders and quickly developed a cadre of influential and strategically placed contacts (McLean, 2000). Supported financially by the CSP, NAMI grew to 15,000 members and 270 affiliated groups in only 5 years. Ten years later, the number of members reached 125,000 and 1,050 affiliates. NAMI now has 220,000 members and 1,200 affiliates (NAMI, 2002). A grassroots effort, NAMI's size and influence has grown by word of mouth and media exposure rather than through paid organizers and traveling staff (Sommer, 1990). A strong sense of self-reliance was created through

NAMI's refusal to accept the unquestioned wisdom of mental health professionals, recognizing from the beginning an inherent conflict of interest in the attitude and approach of these professionals. To this day, unless professionals have mentally ill relatives, they are not allowed to serve on the NAMI board of directors, in stark contrast to their dominance within earlier mental health organizations (Hatfield, 1991).

Although NAMI began as a volunteer effort with members doing everything, volunteers inevitably became overburdened as the organization rapidly grew. NAMI began hiring staff in its second year, and had approximately 25 paid staff members only a decade later (Hatfield, 1991).

NAMI now operates as a pyramidal organization, with local chapters operating at the city and/or county levels while remaining affiliated with a state organization located in the state capital. The state-level offices are affiliated with the national office in Washington, D.C. The organization remains highly decentralized at each geographic level. This decentralization entails the maintenance of separate memberships, newsletters and appeals for funds at local, state and national levels, with all three levels occasionally competing simultaneously for member support. This may be due in part due to NAMI's rapid growth, its grassroots nature, and the distinct type of activities that occur at national, state and local levels.

The national office, with a paid professional and support staff, and an elected board, maintains contacts with members of Congress and executive agencies to ensure federal support for research and treatment initiatives. The office also coordinates direct fundraising and produces and distributes printed materials. Since mental health legislation in the United States is considered to be a state responsibility, the NAMI statewide offices focus on developing and sustaining legislative contacts, advocating for specific treatment programs, and distributing educational materials produced by the national office and other mental health agencies (Sommer, 1990).

NAMI has four primary missions: (1) support for parents and relatives through local direct services, such as the provision of information relating to programs and resources, assistance with legal issues, support for political action, and the organization of meetings and events of interest to the membership; (2) the provision of peer education for NAMI members about treatments, services and research, and the education of media personnel, public officials, healthcare providers, educators, the business community, and the general public about brain disorders; (3) research to yield better treatments, more helpful interventions, and strategies for the prevention of disabling conditions such as schizophrenia and bipolar disorder; and (4) advocacy for changes in laws and policies that deny NAMI members basic protections (Foulks, 2000).

ACT UP

ACT UP (2002) describes itself as "a diverse, non-partisan group of individuals united in anger and committed to direct action to end the AIDS crisis." Its mission is: "We advise and inform. We demonstrate. We are not silent. Silence equals death." The New York Chapter of ACT UP adds the following statements: "We meet with government and health officials; we research and distribute the latest medical information. We protest and demonstrate; we are not silent. We challenge anyone who, by their actions or inaction, hinders the fight against AIDS. This includes those who: don't work for adequate funding or leadership for AIDS research, health care, or housing for people with AIDS; block the dissemination of life-saving information about safer sex, clean needles, and other AIDS prevention; and encourage discrimination against people who are living with AIDS." Using non-violent direct action, including vocal demonstrations and dramatic acts of civil disobedience to focus attention on the AIDS crisis, ACT UP's membership has grown to thousands with more than 70 chapters in the U.S. and worldwide (ACT UP, 2002).

ACT UP was born on March 10, 1987, in the basement of the Lesbian and Gay Community Services Center in New York when activist Larry Kramer was asked to fill in as a substitute speaker. "After looking over the audience of 250 people, he asked about two-thirds of them to stand. When they had, he delivered this grim diagnosis: 'At the rate we are going, you could be dead in less than five years. If my speech tonight doesn't scare the shit out of you, we're in real trouble. If what you're hearing doesn't rouse you to anger, fury, rage, and action, gay men will have no future here on earth. How long does it take before you get angry and fight back?'" Kramer went on to appeal for stronger leadership in political lobbying and advocacy. At a follow-up meeting two days later, several hundred people committed to direct action to end the AIDS crisis gathered and began "to fight back in earnest." Christened ACT UP (AIDS Coalition to Unleash Power), the new organization adopted as its logo the "despised pink triangle worn by homosexuals in the concentration camps of Hitler's Germany," but with the point up and a grim motto underneath: "Silence = Death" (Arno and Feiden, 1992: 73–75).

ACT UP's first demonstration occurred two weeks later, with participants converging on Wall Street to protest the high cost of AZT, the then-miracle drug, and to focus attention on government inaction with respect to AIDS research. Some lay down in front of traffic on Wall and Broad Streets and others hung in effigy then-FDA commissioner, Frank Young, from the gallows in Trinity Church. Seventeen people were arrested (Arno and Feiden, 1992). Shortly afterward, the FDA announced that it would shorten its drug approval process by two years (ACT UP, 2002). For the first time, the "victims" of a disease successfully began to organize a political and investigative revolution, challenging the governmental and medical establishments (Halsall, 1998).

According to Rosenau (1994), ACT UP represents a social movement influenced by a post-modern perspective where culture is sometimes as important as politics. Structural and ideological factors in this type of movement allow diametrically opposed views to be expressed and acted upon. This approach enhances both creativity and innovation and may be key to ACT UP's success in challenging medical and governmental authority and in changing the pharmaceutical approval process. This type of movement emphasizes the impact of the action of authorities on the individual person. ACT-UP's community organizing techniques also employ a post-modern pastiche of ideas, views and strategies, including drama and theater, video and photography, civil disobedience, demonstrations, museum exhibits, direct information, community contacts and outreach, as well as scholarly research.

ACT UP has no board of directors, paid staff, or elected leader. In New York, town hall meetings are held each Monday and a "facilitator" is assigned control of the floor; this position changes regularly. Voting privileges are acquired after attending two sessions, but attendance is not taken. Typically, 400 members attend the meetings, which are characterized by their length (upwards of 5 hours) and the high level of audience participation (Arno and Feiden, 1992).

The "Original Working Document" of ACT UP established a Coordinating Committee to facilitate the administrative functioning of the organization. The Committee is comprised of one representative from each of five committees (Outreach, Logistics, Issues, Media and Fundraising) and four individuals selected by the entire group (secretary, treasurer, and two at-large members). The Coordinating Committee meets as frequently as necessary. Specific work of the Coordinating Committee includes expense authorization between large general meetings, review of materials developed, coordination of the work of the other committees, and planning of the general meeting agenda. The Coordinating Committee is not authorized to elect officers or set policy; all general policies are decided by the body as a whole (ACT UP, 2002).

Over the years, ACT UP's activists mastered the art of the sound bite and pioneered telephone and fax "zaps," in which the lines of target agencies are jammed with hundreds of simultaneous calls. Members have been harsh towards their critics and those deemed enemies of the cause, including New York Mayor Ed Koch, who was shouted down at a gay history exhibit, and former New York City Health Commissioner Stephen C. Joseph, on whose house members of ACT UP splashed paint and pasted handbills after he reduced estimates of the number of HIV-positive individuals from 400,000 to 200,000, based on more refined epidemiological data. AIDS researchers at Harvard were also repeated targets of ACT UP, due to the slow pace of AIDS drug development. During a high mass at St. Patrick's Cathedral, 5,000 protestors gathered to castigate the Catholic Church for its condemnation of homosexuality, its refusal to sanction the protective value of condoms, and its opposition to abortion and safe-sex education. Some of the demonstrators were dressed as bishops, others as clowns, and one man came in the habit of the Flying Nun. Several of the protestors bore a large mock condom which they had named 'Cardinal O'Condom,' Other protestors laid down in the aisles of the cathedral and chained themselves to the pews. One ACT-UP member inside of the cathedral first accepted a communion wafer from Archbishop John Cardinal O'Connor and then crumbled it on the floor, with the statement, "Opposing safe-sex education is murder" (Arno and Feiden, 1992: 77).

ACT UP achieved many of its goals and objectives by staging "spectacular street theater" and "hard backroom work." Although the organization's tactics shocked many, that shock gave the organization its power. However, both ACT UP's press releases and graphics reflected considerable work and research. Members were routinely seen in the late 1980s at the New York Public Library conducting extensive research on a wide array of subjects. ACT UP ultimately had a tremendous and significant influence on public policy, making considerable inroads into the health and medical science establishment bureaucracy. Members of ACT UP graduated from being unwelcome guests "crashing" major scientific meetings and public hearings in their early years to becoming respected invited speakers and presenters. It was instrumental in reducing health insurance costs, in making needle exchange a viable policy, and in transforming the way drugs were assessed. Ultimately, the actions of ACT UP members may have saved thousands of lives (Halsall, 1998).

DISCUSSION QUESTIONS

1.   Describe the differences between a grassroots movement and a "top-down" approach. What are the advantages or disadvantages of each model?

2.   Describe any grassroots efforts in your community. What was the impetus for the movement(s)? Have they been successful? Why or why not? What characteristics described in this chapter do they possess?

REFERENCES

ACT UP (AIDS Coalition to Unleash Power) (2002). New York, NY (January 31, 2002); http://www.actupny.org.

Arno, P.S., & Feiden, K,L. (1992). *Against the Odds: The Story of AIDS, Drug Development, Politics and Profits.* New York: HarperCollins.

Barry, F. (1982). Mobilization of community resources to work with abusive and neglectful families: Community organization in New York State. *Child Abuse and Neglect, 6,* 177–184.

Flick L.H., Reese, C.G., Rogers, G., Fletcher, P., & Sonn J. (1994). Building community for health: lessons from a seven-year-old neighborhood/university partnership. *Health Education Quarterly, 21,* 369–380.

Foulks, E.F. (2000). Advocating for persons who are mentally ill: a history of mutual empowerment of patients and profession. *Administration and Policy in Mental Health, 27,* 353–367.

Halsall, P., ed. (1998). *People With A History: An Online Guide to Lesbian, Gay, Bisexual and Trans History.* New York (March 6, 1998); http://www.fordham.edu.halsall.pwh/.

Hatfield, A.B. (1991). The national alliance for the mentally ill: a decade later. *Community Mental Health Journal, 27,* 95–103.

Johnson, J., Blanchard, J., & Harvey, C. (2000). Americans' view of cancer. *Support Care Cancer, 8,* 24–27.

Labonte, R. (1994). Health promotion and empowerment: reflections on professional practice. *Health Education Quarterly, 21(2),* 253–268.

MADD—Mothers Against Drunk Driving (2002). Dallas, TX (February 12, 2002); http://www.madd.org.

Martin, G.S., Galvan, U., Perini, G.P., & Morgante, S. (1991). An international perspective on organizing people at risk for AIDS at the community level. *Antibiot Chemother., 43,* 257–263.

Mayster, V., Waitzkin, H., Hubbell, F.A., & Rucker, L. (1990). Local advocacy for the medically indigent: Strategies and accomplishments in one county. *Journal of the American Medical Association, 263,* 262–268.

McLean, A.H. (2000). From ex-patient alternatives to consumer options: consequences of consumerism for psychiatric consumers and the ex-patient movement. *International Journal of Health Services, 30,* 821–847.

Merideth, E. (1994). Critical pedagogy and its application to health education: A critical appraisal of the Casa en Casa model. *Health Education Quarterly, 21,* 355–367.

Million Mom March (2002). Washington, D.C. (February 6, 2002); http://www.millionmommarch.com.

Minkler, M. (1978). Ethical issues in community organization. *Health Education Monographs, 6,* 198–210.

Minkler, M. (1985). Building supportive ties and sense of community among the inner-city elderly: The Tenderloin Senior Outreach Project. *Health Education Quarterly, 12,* 303–314.

Minkler, M. (1992). Community organizing among the elderly poor in the United States: A case study. *International Journal of Health Services, 22,* 303–316.

Mosher J.F. (1999). Alcohol policy and the young adult: Establishing priorities, building partnerships, overcoming barriers. *Addiction, 94,* 357–369.

Moss, A.R. (2000). Epidemiology and the politics of needle exchange. *American Journal of Public Health, 90,* 1385–1387.

NAMI (National Alliance for the Mentally Ill) (2002). Arlington, VA (February 12, 2002); http://www.nami.org.

National Mental Health Association (2002). Alexandria, VA (February 14, 2002); http://www.nmha.org.

Rosenau, P.V. (1994). Health politics meets post-modernism: Its meaning and implications for community health organizing. *Journal of Health Politics, Policy and Law, 19*, 303–333.

Sommer, R. (1990). Family advocacy and the mental health system: The recent rise of the Alliance for the Mentally Ill. *Psychiatric Quarterly, 61*, 205–221.

Speer, P.W., & Hughey, J. (1995). Community organizing: An ecological route to empowerment and power. *American Journal of Community Psychology, 23*, 729–748.

Tanner, C.A. (2000). On grassroots activism and health policy: A case study. *Journal of Nursing Education, 39*, 148.

Treno, A.J., & Holder, H.D. (1997a). Community mobilization: Evaluation of an environmental approach to local action. *Addiction, 92*, S173–S187.

Treno, A.J., & Holder, H.D. (1997b). Community mobilization, organizing, and media advocacy. A discussion of methodological issues. *Evaluation Review, 21*, 166–190.

Ugalde, A. (1985). Ideological dimensions of community participation in Latin American health programs. *Social Science and Medicine, 21*, 41–53.

Ungerleider, S., Bloch, S.A. (1988). Perceived effectiveness of drinking-driving countermeasures: An evaluation of MADD. *Journal of Studies on Alcohol, 49*, 191–195.

Wagenaar, A.C., Murray, D.M., Gehan, J.P., Wolfson, M., Forster, J.L., Toomey, T.L., Perry, C.L., & Jones-Webb, R. (2000). Communities mobilizing for change on alcohol: Outcomes from a randomized community trial. *Journal of Studies on Alcohol, 61*, 85–94.

CHAPTER FOUR

Building Coalitions

Nature teaches beasts to know their friends.
(William Shakespeare, *Coriolanus*, II. i, 6)

While grassroots organizing forms the "bedrock" for community health advocacy and policy change, the building of coalitions creates the framework upon that foundation within which to accomplish these ends at local, regional, state and federal levels (Mosher, 1999). Coalition building can often be used to overcome the political limitations of community organizing (Labonte, 1994). Advocacy efforts, on the other hand, may fail due to nonexistent, weak, or fragmented coalitions. This chapter discusses strategies for the formation of multi-sector coalitions and how they can best be utilized in promoting a community health agenda.

Over the past 20 years, community-based coalitions have become popular structures for creating community benefits and interventions for change across America, and this phenomenon continues to evolve (Berkowitz, 2001; Wolff, 2001a). Community coalitions are often formed as a component of health promotion and prevention initiatives to address complex and entrenched social and health problems, such as tobacco use, alcoholism and other substance abuse, maternal and child health, crime (community policing efforts), economic deprivation, school reform, cancer and cardiovascular disease, and the overall revitalization of communities. Coalition initiatives also vary in their geographic scope (for instance, their scope may be at the national, state, region, county, city, neighborhood, and/or school levels), while membership may be limited to public agencies, public and private agencies, multiple sectors, spiritual institutions, business, government, and/or grassroots leaders (Chavis, 1995). Only a small fraction of this work has been documented. Estimates extrapolated from the number of known community coalitions place the total number at several thousand across the country (Berkowitz, 2001).

WHAT ARE COMMUNITY COALITIONS?

"Coalitions are groups of groups with a shared goal and some awareness that 'united we stand, divided we fall'" (Labonte, 1994: 263). They are comprised of individuals representing diverse organizations, institutions, factions or constituencies from multiple sectors of the community that, through communication, coordination, and collaboration, work together to solve community problems (Chavis, 1995). Coalitions have the unique "paradox of participant advocacy and commitment of resources to both the organization they represent and the coalitions themselves" (Chavis, 1995: 235). This creates an inherent conflict and tension within the coalition, particularly in coalitions of groups that are diverse in terms of economic resources and stability.

Wolff (2001a) suggests, in addition, that community coalitions be citizen-influenced if not citizen-driven, that they focus on multiple local issues rather than national issues, and that they address community needs by building community assets. Wolff also envisions community coalitions as being sustained for the long term. Community coalitions have been used to effectuate program, practice, and policy change across a wide range of issues, including economic development, substance abuse, tobacco control, racism, violence prevention, and environmental regulation. Chavis (1995), in a review of the literature on coalitions for disease prevention, suggests that community coalitions are capable of several primary functions: broadening the mission of member organizations to develop more comprehensive strategies; creating broader public support on issues; increasing the influence of individual community institutions over community policies and practices; minimizing duplication of services; developing more financial and human resources; increasing participation from diverse sectors and communities; exploiting new resources in a changing environment; increasing accountability; increasing capacity to plan and evaluate; and strengthening local organizations and institutions to respond better to the needs and aspirations of their constituents.

Community coalitions that are effective (1) are holistic and comprehensive, addressing issues ranging from economics to the environment and acknowledging interconnections between them; (2) are flexible and responsive to emerging issues and new community needs; (3) build a sense of community and a sense of belonging; (4) build and enhance resident engagement in community life; (5) provide a vehicle for community empowerment; (6) value and celebrate diversity; and (7) generate innovative solutions to large problems facing not only their community, but also the nation as a whole (Wolff, 2001a).

STRATEGIES FOR THE FORMATION OF
MULTI-LEVEL COALITIONS

Creating a Community Coalition: External Factors

The internal and external variables that lead to the development and growth of community coalitions are numerous. (Wolff, 2001a) notes several factors that have fostered widespread development of community coalitions across the country. These include: (1) the expansion of interventions from targeted initiatives focused on specific problems to a wide range of public health concerns affecting the larger community; (2) the devolution or shift in financial and program responsibility of federal programs to local government, often accompanied by the inadequate allocation of dollars to the local communities; (3) the need to do more with less, reflective of shrinking government resources for basic health and human needs coupled with the expectation that communities become more cost effective and productive; (4) limitations of the health and human service system, which is often too fragmented, bureaucratic, insensitive, inaccessible, and complex to address effectively a community's needs; and (5) a decline of civic engagement with key institutions, including schools, churches, police and elected and non-elected officials, in local communities out of touch with their constituencies.

Wolff (2001b) suggests that community coalitions will most likely continue to be powerful forces for addressing needs and gaps and creating community change. Community coalitions are at the heart of the transition from a government-dominated model to a community empowerment model. According to Kurland and Zeder (2001), however, coalition building, rather than taking over the role of government, empowers communities to build their own futures.

Creating a Community Coalition: Requisite Elements

Folayemi (2001) has identified ten key ingredients necessary for the creation of coalitions: (1) patience in addressing a diverse range of backgrounds, interests, agendas and perspectives; (2) effective communication; (3) a focus on the larger goals, the problem and the community;

(4) broad-based participation, allowing for a more comprehensive solution and a sense of ownership for all; (5) technical assistance so that everyone understands the process; (6) respect for a diversity of opinion; (7) adaptability; (8) trust in the skills and commitment that each individual or organization brings to the process; (9) a recognition of shortcomings and mistakes as well as successes; and (10) commitment to the community being served and the broader goal to be attained, in lieu of an investment in personal egos or agendas.

Although often successful as vehicles for community change, many community coalitions fail to develop and achieve their goals, wasting time and energy in the process. Wolff (2001c) explores nine dimensions that he believes are critical to building successful coalitions: community readiness, intentionality, structure and organizational capacity, taking action, membership, leadership, dollars and resources, relationships, and technical assistance. Following is a brief summary of each.

Community Readiness

Community readiness prior to the creation of the coalition is critical. Readiness refers to the ability of the community to identify mechanisms to solve its own problems. The impetus should come from within the community, rather than outside (government, foundations, etc.). Community ownership increases with internal impetus, although external impetus may offer needed resources. Past successes with collaborations will invariably make the process easier than in communities that have not had that history. The extent of conflict or "turf wars" between and within community groups may create possibly insurmountable difficulties in developing the coalition. It may also be more difficult in communities that are "overcoalitioned," or already have multiple coalitions. This is increasingly the case in some communities due to requirements of government or foundations to receive funding. The quality of available leaders is also critical.

Intentionality

Intentionality is the common shared vision and mission, which must be clear to all participants and be directly related to the group's goals, objectives, and day-to-day activities. Goals and objectives must be concrete, attainable, and measurable. As a "bottom-up" approach, community members are at the core, empowered by defining the mission, vision, goals and objectives, identifying the issues, analyzing the problems, selecting the interventions, and delivering the interventions and evaluation themselves. Empowered members have greater faith in themselves to take on issues and resolve them. Successful coalitions allow the members them- selves to envision and create the future of both the community and the coalition.

Structure and Organizational Capacity

The organization must have the capacity to make decisions, commu- nicate, raise and maintain resources, and provide leadership. Paid staff for the coalition, while often unpopular with coalitions that arise from grassroots volunteer efforts, are often necessary to produce expected re- sults, particularly in dealing with numerous issues, and to keep members engaged. Decisionmaking in a coalition is frequently complex and often requires shared responsibility for the decisions across a wide number of groups, such as coalition staff, committees, task forces, membership, out- side funders, and/or a lead agency. Roles and responsibilities across the core responsibilities (spending money, hiring, setting direction) must be clearly spelled out and understood across the coalition membership. Coalitions build ownership and trust by ensuring that all members are aware and understand the actions of the coalition. Externally, coalitions build power and respect by highlighting activities and accomplishments. Newsletters and well-designed meetings can enhance communication.

Taking Action

Taking action within the coalition's vision and mission and keeping it in the forefront is critical to creating community change, and to building and sustaining membership. Coalitions rely on the volunteer support and participation of its members, while members rely on coalitions to achieve changes that they cannot achieve themselves. Achievement and documen- tation of concrete outcomes are important not only to members, but also to evaluators and funders. Coalitions must have the capacity to address change both within the community (for new local programs, policies, and practices) and outside of it (addressing funding policies, programs, and practices at the state or federal level). This often requires advocacy, which may or may not include confrontational strategies. This may be consid- ered counter to the coalition concept of collaboration and some fear that this may limit capacity to create community change. Coalition building requires both advocacy and relationship-building, i.e., power-based and relationship-based change, but coalitions must also be careful to distin- guish between the two, and use each as appropriate. Advocacy requires the transformation and redistribution of power. A relationship-based approach effectuates change by building strong, caring, and respectful relationships among community members. Successful coalitions create working task forces that set clear goals, objectives and realistic work plans, including measurable indicators of success. Action plans and timelines for the coalition as a whole and for its task forces are reviewed on a regular basis by the leadership to ensure action. The coalition routinely publicizes its actions internally and externally.

Membership

Membership representing a broad cross-section of the community is essential to success. Membership should be defined first and foremost by involvement and participation in coalition activities, whether financial resources or just endorsement of the mission and goals are required. Membership recruitment must be ongoing, with leaders and other members identifying new players from within or outside of the community to participate in various coalition activities. Membership recruitment should strive toward openness and inclusivity, engaging all residents and key leaders of a community. Diversity in membership should be an essential goal of the coalition; this can be defined by race, culture, gender, age, geographic location, etc. Groups that are targeted by the work of the coalition should be represented or brought to the table. Representatives of both the least and the most powerful members of the community should be engaged in the ownership and sharing of power within the coalition. The balancing of these factors and interests is challenging but, if accomplished, will provide members with a sense of ownership in the processes, accomplishments, and failures of the coalition. Successful coalitions understand that individuals join because they are personally invited and are nurtured in their membership through the receipt of recognition, respect, reward, the formation of relationships, and the achievement of results. The payoff is increased participation.

Leadership

Leadership in successful coalitions is collaborative, dispersed and developed among all members of the coalition. Leaders must be flexible, trustworthy and patient; they must see the "big picture," offering energy and hope to the vision and actions of the coalition. They are also skilled in conflict resolution, communication, group facilitation, modeling and nurturing leadership in others, and fostering commitment at all levels. Collaborative leaders inspire others, sustain hope, help to solve problems, share power, and focus on facilitation and process. They are flexible in their approach, inclusive of others, proactive, and concerned with the whole, rather than component parts. Successful coalitions strive to develop and expand leadership among their members.

Funding

The level of funding and the decision-making process with respect to the use of those funds may affect the nature of the coalition. The availability of funding is not a guarantee of success; there have been successful coalitions with little funding and also well-funded coalitions that have failed. The availability or promise of resources is often a factor in the creation of some coalitions, while other grassroots groups may begin without any funding. Initial and even sustained community ownership and involvement tends to be more reliably present in the latter.

Funding support usually begins by covering the basic office supplies and staff, and is then used to address specific programs. The integrity and authenticity of the coalition must be balanced with the needs and requirements of funders; one must consider whether the coalition's agenda is determined by the extent and source of the funding or by the coalition's mission. The intense search and competition for limited resources is time- and personnel-intensive. Even when successful, it may be extremely difficult to sustain the funding for any period of time. This is, in part, due to government's failure to perceive community needs holistically; categorical funding tends to splinter resources among competing community and other government entities.

Relationships

Relationships are the building blocks of coalitions, bringing people together to foster collective problem-solving to improve quality of life in the community. Conflicts are inherent in encouraging relationships across a diverse spectrum of the community. The coalition must be a safe environment that allows conflicts to surface and be managed constructively. Connections of members within the coalition can also create spin-off benefits outside the coalition, including socialization, information sharing, collaborative funding proposals, cross referrals, and joint project design. Successful coalitions create opportunities to share through annual dinners and other events, and encourage informal meetings to read and share ideas with one another.

Technical Assistance

Technical assistance in the form of consultation, training, and support for coalition staff, boards, and members is often critical to build coalitions successfully. Other established coalitions can provide peer support and sample goals, objectives, job descriptions, and budgets. Written materials, manuals, tip sheets, websites, and other resources are also available. Coalition building requires staff, boards and members to set their scope on the whole community in all of its diversity, engage all sectors, and create community change on a multitude of fronts simultaneously, and often with extremely limited resources. Without planned technical assistance and support, successful and sustained coalition building is challenging even under the best of circumstances.

Collaborative Capacity

Collaborative capacity, consisting of member, relational, organizational, and programmatic capacities, is a prerequisite for the effectuation of sustainable community change (Foster-Fishman, Berkowitz, Lounsbury, Jacobson and Allen, 2001).

Building Member Capacity To Collaborate. Building member capacity to collaborate requires the development of (1) core skills and knowledge to work collaboratively with others, to create and build effective programs, and to build an effective coalition infrastructure; (2) positive attitudes about the need for and value of collaboration, the proposed project or issue to be addressed, the other stakeholders, and the roles of those participating in the coalition; and (3) a diverse membership and support for that diversity.

Creating Relational Capacity

This entails the creation of positive internal relationships through a shared vision, a positive working atmosphere, and an inclusive culture, as well as the creation of positive external relationships with organizational sectors, entities, and individuals that are not represented in the coalition, in order to access a broad array of resources and to facilitate a shared vision.

Building Organizational Capacity

Building organizational capacity to engage members and produce desired products requires the following characteristics: (1) strong current and emerging leaders who have the requisite skills, relationships, and vision to motivate individuals to transcend their individual interests in favor of a common goal; (2) well-defined staff and member roles and responsibilities and clear guidelines to achieve goals and objectives; (3) effective internal communication patterns that encourage discussion about problems and the identification of suitable resolutions; (4) adequate human and financial resources; and (5) an orientation to continuous learning, feedback and evaluation, and utilization of external information and expertise.

Programmatic Capacity. Programmatic capacity refers to the identification of community needs, the creation of innovative solutions, and the mobilization of community support through the formulation of clear, focused programmatic objectives. As an example, the effectiveness of culturally competent programs rests on the alignment of their programmatic components with the unique cultural values, attitudes, language, and behaviors of the populations to which they are geared.

Creating Coalition Partnerships

Successful coalitions are built through effective partnerships. Labonte (1994) has identified the following nine characteristics of effective partnerships. (1) each partner has established its own power and legitimacy; (2) each partner has a well-defined mission statement; (3) each partner respects the autonomy of the other coalition members and recognizes that the common goal is larger than any of the goals held by the individual organization members; (4) each partner is well-rooted in its relevant community and is accountable to an identifiable constituency; (5) institutional partners are committed to working together in a partnership with community groups; (6) the partners have developed clear objectives and expectations; (7) the partners have drafted written agreements that clearly set forth the parties' objectives and responsibilities and the standards to be upheld; (8) the community group partners have the support of community workers; and (9) each partner strives for openmindedness, patience, and respect.

COALITIONS IN ACTION

Local Coalitions

The Pro-Youth Coalition (PYC)

The Pro-Youth Coalition (PYC) in Santa Barbara County, described by Folayemi (2001), consists of over 60 partners representing a spectrum of private, public, nonprofit and faith-based organizations. Its grassroots membership, the General Body of the coalition, decides all major financial and programmatic issues. Leadership is fostered and developed from among its grassroots constituency. Many of its initiatives were developed out of issues raised in support groups composed of youth and parents, PYC's target population.

The Orange County Task Force On Indigent Health Care

Mayster and colleagues (1990) report several strategies used by a community-based coalition, coordinated by the Orange County Task Force On Indigent Health Care, to improve access to care for the medically indigent, including research, and political and legal strategies. These efforts significantly improved the availability of local services. The coalition comprises various organizations with different constituencies; each member organization is concerned about health care access. The coalition has had success in lobbying the Board of Supervisors and Orange County Health Care Agency staff to expand county-funded prenatal care. The coalition also successfully targeted the University of California, Irvine Medical Center to prevent a takeover by a for-profit hospital chain that refused to assure continued access for publicly insured or uninsured patients. Pressure from the coalition also reversed proposals by university officials for new cutbacks and financial barriers.

De Madres a Madres

Another successful community coalition is De Madres a Madres in Houston, Texas (McFarlane, Kelly, Rodriguez and Fehir, 1994). An outreach network was formed with community businesses, health and social service agencies, schools, and churches to encourage pregnant Mexican-American women to obtain early prenatal care. The effort, sponsored by the March of Dimes and Texas Woman's University, was premised on the concepts of community awareness, volunteerism, and the empowerment of women and a strategy comprised of group decision making, shared power, the enhancement of individual worth and dignity, and the positive use of risk taking. Coalitions were formed of women willing to assist women in reducing their personal isolation and to address language- and immigration-related barriers to accessing care. The women, who named the program "De Madres a Madres" ("From Mothers to Mothers"), recruited volunteers to promote support between mothers for at-risk pregnant Hispanic women through personal contact, in-home visits, assessments of family needs, the provision of community referrals, the provision of emotional support, and the sharing of experiences.

The volunteers were recognized and respected as experts and were sought out by both leaders and residents. They have successfully lobbied city council and local legislatures to expand clinic hours and facilitate access for the women, and a center for the program recently opened. De Madres a Madres has formed several coalitions with other community entities to offer a variety of other services for the women. As a result of the program, the women are involved in their community, are better able to define their own issues and goals, and their right to quality health care has been validated.

The Worcester AIDS Consortium

A study by Zapka, Marrocco, Lewis, McCusker, Sullivan, McCarthy and Birch (1992) presents the development of the Worcester (Massachusetts) AIDS Consortium as an example of a successful intra-organizational collaboration based on resource development needs. Founded in 1987 to provide HIV/AIDS education and risk reduction targeted to intravenous drug users (IVDUs) and their sexual partners, it has expanded to include a wide range of programs and activities. The early leadership was proactive in acknowledging that while each member organization has its own goals, service domain, and needs, the coalition as a whole had greater power than the individual members and could be more successful in developing and sustaining resources. Each member agency is also more successful in achieving its respective goals by working with others than by working independently. Funds were to flow through one organization, the Worcester Health Department. Other key leaders also provide some balance of power within the Consortium. Inevitable tensions and conflicts are not perceived as impeding the work of the Consortium, but rather as part of Consortium process and maintenance.

State and National Coalitions

The Coalition for a Healthy California

Najera (1998) describes the coalition-building process around a tobacco tax ballot initiative in California. Although earlier efforts to place similar propositions on the state ballot in 1978 and 1980 failed due to the tobacco industry's formidable influence and well-funded campaigns, the public mood had shifted dramatically by 1987. The American Lung Association, working with Assemblyman Lloyd Connelly, led efforts to establish the Coalition for a Healthy California. Its structure included an Executive Committee (policy body), and an advisory Steering Committee. The Executive Committee conducted day-to-day decision-making. The Coalition included a total of 22 statewide organizations and over 300 individual members, representatives of public and private agencies, businesses, educators, elected officials, and private individuals. Each organizational member committed to the use of its name in the anti-tobacco campaign, the provision of education related to coalition building to its membership, and participation in the campaign to the extent possible.

The Executive Committee initially included representatives from the American Cancer Society, the American Lung Association of California, the Planning and Conservation League, the Campaign for California Committee, and Assemblyman Lloyd Connelly. The California Medical Association, the California Association of Hospitals and Health Systems, and the American Heart Association joined five months later. The doctors and hospitals were recruited after it was acknowledged that additional political strength and financing were needed; to accomplish this, the Coalition negotiated a large share of the anticipated revenue from the new cigarette tax to go to doctors and hospitals. Although the Coalition members were united in the belief that smoking was a bad health practice and that consumption could be cut by increasing the price of tobacco products, the interests of Coalition members varied significantly in who should benefit from the tax revenue. Doctors and hospitals wanted to increase funding for health care for the poor. The American Cancer Society and the American Lung Association preferred to target funding for the tobacco health education fund, to educate people and discourage smoking, and to finance tobacco-related research. The issue was never fully resolved.

Some important lessons were learned from the experience. Significant work remained following the successful ballot initiative; this work required that the Coalition remain united through this phase as well. Coalition members must be prepared for controversy. The Coalition must be careful in its negotiations to assure that the initiative message reflects what the voters want, must be aware of opposing viewpoints, and must be willing and able to address and eliminate its own vulnerabilities.

Coalitions for Mentally Ill Persons and Their Families

Foulks (2000) notes the long history of coalitions in advocating for and empowering persons who are mentally ill and their family members. Collaborations among professionals, consumers and concerned citizens in mental health advocacy have existed for more than 150 years. For example, leaders in psychiatry often work with non-professional advocacy groups like the National Mental Health Association or National Alliance for the Mentally Ill for local community awareness and development projects. These include Mental Illness Awards Week (MIAW) programs, radio and TV talk shows, newspaper editorials, and fundraising events. The combination of expert knowledge and the self-disclosure of mentally ill persons and their family members is both persuasive and effective. By working together, the professionals and nonprofessionals reduce the likelihood that those with opposing interests will be able to "divide and conquer."

The National SAFE KIDS Campaign

The National SAFE KIDS Campaign was begun in 1988 by the Children's National Medical Center in Washington, D.C. It is the first and only nationwide injury prevention program (Crawley, Chaloupka, and Kelker, 1994) targeting injuries due to motor vehicle crashes, bike crashes, pedestrian injuries, fires, burns, falls, poisonings, and drownings. As the leading cause of death among children in the United States, preventable injury kills more than 8,000 children each year and results in the permanent disability of 50,000 more.

The national office of SAFE KIDS in Washington, D.C. offers assistance in the development of targeted prevention strategies, the provision of informational and financial resources, the initiation of state and local coalitions, and the coordination of national media efforts. At the state and local levels, more than 144 SAFE KIDS coalitions work to create and ensure safer environments for children and to increase parental awareness regarding preventable injuries and the importance of using bicycle helmets, car seats, smoke detectors, and window guard installations. The coalitions are also involved in legislative and regulatory advocacy efforts to protect children. These work-intensive activities are supported by dedicated volunteers committed to stopping preventable deaths of children.

A COALITION IN ACTION: THE HEALTHY MOTHERS, HEALTHY BABIES COALITION

The Healthy Mothers, Healthy Babies Coalition (HMHB), is presented as a case study for a national multi-level coalition (Arkin,1986; National Healthy Mothers, Healthy Babies Coalition, 2002).

HMHB began in 1981, following a conference on infant mortality sponsored by the U.S. Surgeon General. The initial coalition membership, consisting of representatives of six organizations (the American College of Obstetricians and Gynecologists (ACOG), the March of Dimes, the American Academy of Pediatrics, the American Nurses Association, the

National Congress of Parents and Teachers, and the U.S. Public Health Service), was formed to improve the quality and reach of public and professional education related to prenatal and infant care. Continuing as a forum for information exchange and collaboration, HMHB has grown to approximately 100 national voluntary, health professional, and governmental organizational members and 98 State and local HMHB Coalitions across the country. As such, it brings together grassroots maternal and child health efforts of community leaders, health professionals, and families (National Healthy Mothers, Healthy Babies Coalition, 2002).

In 1985, the Department of Health and Human Services, Maternal and Child Health Bureau (MCHB) awarded HMHB a Special Project of Regional and National Significance (SPRANS) grant to support its programs. HMHB subsequently established its Executive Secretariat at ACOG. HMHB gradually expanded its focus by promoting maternal and child health through networking with health professionals and communities at the national, state and community levels (National Healthy Mothers, Healthy Babies Coalition, 2002). The Coalition thereafter began activities related to breastfeeding, substance use, injury prevention, genetics, oral health, and adolescent pregnancy. Educational materials on these topics, a quarterly newsletter and other coalition-building materials (exhibit, slide-tape show, television production kit, and a community organization guide) are produced through in-kind contributions of the organizational members of the coalition. State and community enthusiasm for the HMHB concept, the availability of technical assistance from national members, and support through co-sponsorship of regional conferences, has led to the formation of coalitions in more than 40 states. The state coalitions in turn have undertaken a variety of campaigns, and innovative programs are recognized through annual national HMHB achievement awards (Arkin, 1986).

National membership requires only a nonprofit status, a national network of affiliates, and an interest in maternal and infant health. The national coalition limits its activities to awareness and education, avoiding advocacy for any particular position or issue. This has allowed participation by diverse organizations with a wide range of constituencies and divergent opinions (Arkin, 1986).

The Coalition is managed by the policy subcommittee. Volunteer members of the policy subcommittee include representatives of the member organizations and chairpersons of other Coalition subcommittees. HMHB's Executive Secretariat and the Executive Director oversee day-to-day Coalition business and activities. The Executive Secretariat coordinates subcommittee work, promotes exposure of HMHB and its principles on national and state levels, and coordinates an annual competition for the HMHB national achievement awards, which recognize outstanding or innovative efforts in coalition-building, single awareness-raising events, and ongoing educational campaigns. The National Steering Committee, consisting of representatives of approximately 50 organizations, is charged with oversight responsibility for seven program-directed subcommittees. These subcommittees, comprised of volunteers who develop projects through their personal time commitments and the contributed services and funding from participating organizations, conduct most of HMHB's educational activities. The structure facilitates program development through the sharing of expertise available from groups with a common interest, a group interest in education, and reliance on the diverse Coalition membership for project dissemination. Although subcommittees themselves have no base of funding, the pooling of resources among subcommittee members expands the ability of member organizations to begin new programs, or strengthen existing ones (Arkin, 1986).

Funding supports the Executive Director, a part-time secretary, and a small discretionary budget. In-kind support is provided by the Public Health Service and the American College of Obstetricians and Gynecologists. The bulk of financial support for HMHB activities comes from member contributions and solicitations from the private sector for specific projects (Arkin, 1986).

HMHB was incorporated with its first Board of Directors taking office in 1990. Although these actions were contrary to the original organizational intent to maintain an informal structure, achievement of non-profit corporate status enabled it to access funding sources critically needed to support its growth. In 2000, HMHB created a new 2001–2003 Strategic Plan with a revised mission and seven new goals "to help focus the priority issues of the Coalition and advance its technological capabilities" (National Healthy Mothers, Healthy Babies Coalition, 2002).

The strength and enthusiasm of HMHB's membership is attributable to the progress that has been made towards the fulfillment of its goals and the neutral setting for the discussion of and action with respect to issues of mutual interest. The continued momentum of the organization is a function of the collaborative contacts and the sharing of information, programs, skills, and resources made possible by the coalition (Arkin, 1986).

DISCUSSION QUESTIONS

1.   Describe the characteristics of a coalition likely to be successfully established and sustained. What are the characteristics of a coalition more likely to fail?

2.   How would you go about forming a community coalition to address the shortage of affordable low-income housing in your community? How would you envision progress after one year? Two years? How would you evaluate its success?

REFERENCES

Arkin, E.B. (1986). The Healthy Mothers, Healthy Babies Coalition: Four years of progress. *Public Health Reports, 101*, 147–156.

Berkowitz, B. (2001). Studying the outcomes of community-based coalitions. *American Journal of Community Psychology., 29*, 213–227.

Chavis, D.M. (1995). Building community capacity to prevent violence through coalitions and partnerships. *Journal of Health Care for the Poor and Underserved, 6*, 234–245.

Crawley, T., Chaloupka, M.M., & Kelker, D.B. (1994). Injury prevention symposium. *Journal of Neuroscience Nursing, 26*, 103–106.

Folayemi, B. (2001). Case story #1: Building the grassroots coalition. *American Journal of Community Psychology, 29*, 193–197.

Foster-Fishman, P.G., Berkowitz, S.L., Lounsbury, D.W., Jacobson, S., & Allen, N.A. (2001). Building collaborative capacity in community coalitions: A review and integrative framework. *American Journal of Community Psychology, 29*, 241–261.

Foulks, E.F. (2000). Advocating for persons who are mentally ill: A history of mutual empowerment of patients and profession. *Administration and Policy in Mental Health, 27*, 353–367.

Kurland, J., & Zeder, J. (2001). Coalition-building: The promise of government. *American Journal of Community Psychology, 29*, 285–291.

Labonte, R. (1994). Health promotion and empowerment: Reflections on professional practice. *Health Education Quarterly, 21*, 253–268.

Mayster, V., Waitzkin, H., Hubbell, F.A., & Rucker, L. (1990). Local advocacy for the medically indigent: Strategies and accomplishments in one county. *Journal of the American Medical Association, 263*, 262–268.

McFarlane, J., Kelly, E., Rodriguez, R., & Fehir, J. (1994). De Madres a Madres: Women building community coalitions for health. *Health Care for Women International, 15*, 465–476.

Mosher J.F. (1999). Alcohol policy and the young adult: Establishing priorities, building partnerships, overcoming barriers. *Addiction, 94*, 357–369.

Najera, A.P. (1998). History of successful ballot initiatives—California. *Cancer, 83*, 2680–2684.

National Healthy Mothers, Healthy Babies Coalition (2002). Alexandria, VA (January 12, 2002); http://www.hmhb.org.

Wolff, T. (2001a). Community coalition building—contemporary practice and research: Introduction. *American Journal of Community Psychology, 29*, 165–172.

Wolff, T. (2001b). The future of community coalition building. *American Journal of Community Psychology, 29*, 263–268.

Wolff, T. (2001c). A practitioner's guide to successful coalitions. *American Journal of Community Psychology, 29*, 173–191.

Zapka, J.G., Marrocco, G.R., Lewis, B., McCusker, J., Sullivan, J., McCarthy, J., Birch, F.X. (1992). Inter-organizational responses to AIDS: A case study of the Worcester AIDS Consortium. *Health Education Research, 7*, 31–46.

CHAPTER FIVE

Legislative Advocacy

No one pretends that democracy is perfect or all-wise. Indeed, it has been said that
democracy is the worst form of Government except all those other forms that have been
tried from time to time
(Churchill, 1947).

Numerous additional strategies, using more formal processes, can also be utilized to effectuate change. Legislative advocacy, that is, reliance on the state or federal legislative process, is one such mechanism. A review of the functions of the legislature, in relation to agencies and to the courts, is helpful in understanding how this process can be utilized.

THE LEGAL SYSTEM: AN OVERVIEW

Domains of Law

Law is frequently classified into two domains, the public and the private. Public law encompasses law that is concerned with government or its relations with individuals and businesses. Public law is concerned with the definition, regulation, and enforcement of rights where an entity of the government is a party to the action. Public law derives from constitutions, statutes, and regulations and rules that have been promulgated by an administrative entity, such as a federal agency. For instance, the regulations of the Food and Drug Administration with respect to informed consent would be classified as public law.

Private law refers to law that regulates the relations between and among individuals and businesses. This includes actions relating to contracts, to property matters, and to torts. The primary sources of private law include statutes and judicial decisions.

Law is also classified into criminal and civil law. Criminal law deals with crimes. Even though a crime may have been committed against a person, for instance, when a person is robbed, the crime is said to have been against the state and it is the state (or federal government, depending upon the nature of the crime and the basis of the charge) that has the right to prosecute the accused individual or entity. Civil law is that law that refers to non-criminal public and private law.

Sources of Law

The sources of law can be thought of as being in an inverted pyramidal shape. At the very base of this inverted pyramid is the constitution. Everything above the constitution must be consistent with the principles enunciated in the constitution. Above the constitution are the statutes. As you move up the inverted pyramid, you find the regulations and the precepts that have been derived from cases heard by the court. At each level, the decisions and principles must be consistent with those of the previous levels. Although it would seem that the system is relatively unstable because the constitution, which forms the basis for everything else, is at the point of the pyramid, it is actually quite stable because everything else must remain in balance with the constitution.

The Constitution

The federal constitution has been called the "supreme law of the land." The Constitution actually represents a grant of power from the states to the federal government because all powers not specifically delegated to the federal government are, pursuant to the terms of the Constitution, reserved to the states.

The Constitution allocates power among three branches of government. The legislative branch is charged with the responsibility and delegated the authority to make laws (statutes). The executive branch of the government is responsible for the enforcement of the laws, while the judicial branch is responsible for the interpretation of those laws.

There are 26 amendments to the main body of the Constitution. The first 10 of these amendments are known as the Bill of Rights. These encompass many of the rights with which people may be most familiar, such as freedom of speech and freedom of religion. It is important to remember, though, that these rights as delineated are in the federal constitution and as such apply to the federal, not state, government. The Fourteenth Amendment, however, provides specifically that no state may deprive any person of life, liberty, or property without the due process of law. The Amendment also provides that no state may deny equal protection to any person within its jurisdiction. Most of the rights that are enumerated in the Bill of Rights have been found by the Supreme Court to constitute due process, so that ultimately, these rights also apply to the states as well as to the federal government.

Each of the 50 states also has its own constitution. The state constitutions cannot grant to persons fewer rights than are guaranteed to them by the federal constitution. However, they may grant more rights than are provided for by the federal constitution.

Statutes

Statutes at the federal level are promulgated by Congress, consisting of the House of Representatives and the Senate. At the state level, the state legislatures, also consisting of two houses, are responsible for the promulgation of statutes. For example, Congress passed the laws which give the Food and Drug Administration and the Department of Health and Human Services their authority to make regulations. Judges are responsible for the interpretation of the statutes where there is a lack of clarity or where there is conflict between various statutory provisions. This chapter focuses on advocacy in the legislative arena, where statutes are promulgated.

Administrative Law

Administrative law is that law that is made by the agencies which comprise a part of the executive branch of government. Administrative law encompasses regulations, rules, guidelines, and policy memoranda. Examples of administrative agencies relevant to the health advocacy context include the Food and Drug Administration, the National Institutes of Health, and the Department of Health and Human Services. Stated simplistically, an agency's regulations are developed and promulgated through a notice and comment procedure, whereby the proposed regulation is published in the *Federal Register*, which is available to the public for review. Following a mandated time period during which the promulgating agency may receive comments on its proposed regulation, the comment period will cease. After reviewing the comments and incorporating those that the agency deems appropriate, the agency will issue its final regulation. A similar process is followed on the state level. Advocacy in the regulatory context is discussed more fully in chapter 6.

Court Decisions

The use of the courts as an advocacy strategy is discussed in greater depth in chapter 7. However, a basic understanding of how the courts function is helpful here. As indicated, judicial decisions must be consistent with statutes and the Constitution. The courts adhere to the doctrine known as *stare decisis*, meaning that they must look to past cases with similar facts and legal issues to resolve the cases that appear before them. In general, they are bound by decisions of all higher courts within the same jurisdiction. This will become clearer following a discussion of the structure of the legal system. For instance, all federal and state courts are bound by the decisions of the Supreme Court of the United States. All federal district courts are bound by the decisions of the federal Court of Appeal for the circuit in which the federal district court sits, but they are not bound by the decisions of a Court of Appeal for a different circuit. For instance, California sits in the Ninth Circuit. The federal district court for the southern district of California is bound by the decisions of the Ninth Circuit Court of Appeal, but is not bound by the decisions of the Fifth Circuit, which covers the geographic area encompassing such states as Texas and Louisiana.

Judicial decisions also follow the doctrine of *res judicata*. This means that once a case had been decided and all of the channels for appeal have been utilized, the party bringing the case may not bring it again.

LEGISLATURES

The structure, functioning, and derivation of authority of legislatures is similar, but not specifically the same, at the federal and state levels of government. Accordingly, this discussion focuses on the federal legislature and the promulgation of legislation at the federal level. It is important to understand this structure and function in order to advocate effectively at the legislative level.

Legislative Authority

The existence, structure, and functions of our federal Congress derive from the federal Constitution. Congress is charged by the Constitution with the power and authority to provide for the common defense and general welfare, to tax, to regulate the economy, to create courts and military forces, to declare war, and to ratify treaties. The Constitution further specifies that Congress may not perform certain functions, such as taxing state exports, passing bills of attainder (legislation that declares someone guilty of a crime without having had a trial), or adopt *ex post facto* laws (legislation that modifies the legal standing of a past action or event).

Power, however, to enact legislation is shared by three institutions. Two of these institutions, the House of Representatives and the Senate, comprise Congress. The third institution is that of the presidency. This structure provides a mechanism of both direct (the House of Representatives) and indirect (the Senate) representation. Additionally, the legitimacy of the actions taken by Congress and the president are subject to review by the judicial system, in order to ensure that the actions taken are consistent with the precepts of the Constitution (*Marbury v. Madison*, 1803).

Formulating Legislation

Congressional Action

The formulation of proposed legislation may occur in any of several ways. First, a legislator may draft the legislation on his or her own and seek to have the legislation passed by both houses of Congress. Alternatively, the legislation may originate through the action of a citizen or a concerned group, which then approaches a representative in Congress to have the idea introduced in the form of proposed legislation (Sinclair, 1997). Instead of drafting a specific bill, the ideas can also be incorporated into legislation that is being drafted by a legislative committee or they can be offered as an amendment to someone's legislation.

Regardless of how the ideas for a bill are formulated, the legislation itself must be introduced by a member of Congress. This can be done in either the House of Representatives or the Senate. The bill will be assigned a number, but may also be known by a title (Smith, 1995). After the bill is introduced into one of the houses of Congress, it will be sent by the presiding officer of the house into which it was introduced to the appropriate committee. Depending upon the subject matter of the bill, it may be sent to several committees, a process known as multiple referral. This occurs where the bill relates to matters over which several committees may share jurisdiction. Often, the legislation will be sent to a subcommittee of a full committee. Committees and subcommittees have the authority to conduct investigations and hearings, during which they may receive testimony from interested parties and experts.

Committees may also perform markups on legislation, which means that they consider the proposed legislation in detail and amend it as they deem necessary. The committee may then report back the measure to the full House or Senate, but can only do so if a majority of the committee's members are present at the time. The committee must provide a report in reporting back the bill. These reports are frequently written by committee staff members and will often include a minority viewpoint (Smith, 1995).

Committees also have the option of inaction, that is, refusing to act on proposed legislation. When this happens, the legislation is said to have died in committee.

The general process following committee consideration, amendment, and markup consists of the consideration of the proposed legislation on the floor of the house in which it is being considered. The final version of a bill as it is approved by one house of Congress is known as an engrossed bill (Smith, 1995). The two houses of Congress, however, must approve the legislation before it can be forwarded to the president for executive action. The second house can pass the legislation in the same form as it was passed in the house of origin. Alternatively, the two houses may exchange amendments on the legislation until they can agree. Or, the legislation can be forwarded to a conference committee, which consists of representatives of both houses, who are appointed by committee leaders to attempt to resolve the differences between the houses with respect to the proposed legislation. The final version of the bill that is approved by both houses is known as an enrolled bill. This bill is printed on parchment and is certified by either the Clerk of the House or the Secretary of the Senate, based on which house first passed it. It is then signed by the Speakers of the House and the president pro tempore of the Senate, with space reserved for the president's signature.

That said, procedures for the consideration of legislation on the floor differs between the two houses. In the House of Representatives, when major legislation is being considered, the sponsors of the legislation may request a special rule from the Committee on Rules. If granted, the special rule limits general debate on the legislation to one hour. The order of voting on amendments to the legislation may be structured. Members may be allowed to vote on more than one version of the legislation.

There is no such committee in the Senate. The scheduling of legislation to be heard on the floor of the Senate is done by making a motion to proceed to consider it. The motion to proceed, however, can be debated, sometimes to the point that the legislation is "talked to death." This is known as a filibuster. A filibuster can be stopped through cloture, meaning that, if all of the senators are present, 60 of the 100 senators must support cloture in order to end a filibuster.

Legislation relating to government agencies may be for authorization or for appropriations. Authorizing legislation relates to the agency's organization, and ability to make rules, while appropriations legislation provides the money to carry out these functions. How the agencies may utilize the power that is delegated to them to make rules is discussed in chapter 6.

Executive Action

If Congress is still in session when the legislation is approved by both houses and sent to the president, the president may (1) sign the bill into law, (2) veto the bill and send it back to Congress with a statement detailing his objections to the provisions of the legislation, or (3) do nothing. A two-thirds vote of both houses is necessary to override a presidential veto. If the president chooses to do nothing, the bill will become law at the end of 10 days.

If Congress is scheduled to adjourn within the 10 days, the president has the same courses of action available to him. However, because Congress will not be in session, and therefore cannot override a presidential veto, the bill will die if the president vetoes it or if the president does nothing. The veto of a bill in this manner—by doing nothing—is known as a pocket veto.

Influencing Legislation

Lobbyists and Special Interest Groups

Lobbyists, special interest groups, and individual or organizational advocates for a particular cause or position can potentially play a significant role in the legislative process because, depending on the specifics of a situation, they may be able to convince a member of Congress to put a specific issue on the legislative agenda or keep an issue off of the agenda. A lobbyist has been defined as "someone who is paid to communicate with Congress on behalf of others" (Smith, 1995: 326). The role of lobbyists has been criticized even by members of Congress:

> Unfortunately, there is a widespread perception that Members of the Congress are failing to pursue the public interest and are responding to special interests inside the beltway. In the view of many, Members have lost touch with ordinary Americans, in part because they enjoy an assortment of special perks and privileges that are unavailable to the general public.
>
> Now, I know and I believe deeply that many of my colleagues would not change their view on legislative matters because someone offers to buy them a meal or a gift. But the perception problem is real. And the fact is, many Members of Congress do enjoy special advantages that do not accrue to the ordinary American. And many of these special perks are specifically designed to influence Members in the performance of their official duties.
>
> One prime example . . . is the way that many lobbyists shower Members of Congress with gifts. It is not unusual for lobbyists to give Members free tickets to, say, a show, a concert, a sporting event, and take them out to dinner before the event, buy them a cup of coffee and some nice desserts afterward or maybe a little champagne. Some lobbyists regularly take Members out for lavish meals

at expensive restaurants. Let me add that we do not want to hurt the restaurant business, but this needs to be cleaned up.

Sometimes the lobbyists provide Members with free trips, typically involving stays in luxurious hotels in beautiful places, along with various forms of entertainment, whether it is playing tennis, golf, skiing, you name it.

I know that many of my colleagues feel that Members of Congress would not be influenced by a free dinner or even a luxury trip to the Caribbean. And I concur in that. Members of this body are serious, committed public servants who want to do what is right for their constituents and for the country at large.

However, it seems indisputable that these kinds of gifts have contributed to Americans' deepening distrust of Government, and Congress, in particular. And that is a serious problem, for as public trust diminishes, the ability of Congress to address our Nation's serious problems is also diminished (Lautenberg, 1993: S5502).

Special interest groups often include occupational organizations or particular segments of the population. Approximately 20 percent of the interest groups consist of citizens' groups. Such groups

usually arise in the wake of broad social movements concerned with such problems as the level of environmental pollution, threats to civil rights, or changes in the status of women. The groups formed to act as representatives of these social movements often are created by political enterpreneurs operating with the support of wealthy individuals, private foundations, or elected political leaders who act as their protectors, financial supporters, and patrons (Walker, 1991: 10).

A 1986 survey of special interest groups found that more than three-quarters of them employed *all* of the following strategies in their attempts to influence legislation: testifying at hearings, contacting government officials directly, engaging in informal contacts with government officials such as at conventions, presenting research findings or technical information, sending letters to organization members to inform them about activities, entering into coalitions with other organizations, attempting to influence the implementation of policy, interacting with media representatives, consulting with government officials to plan legislative strategy, assisting in drafting legislation, participating in letter writing campaigns, organizing grassroots lobbying efforts, and prevailing upon influential constituents to contact the offices of their local representatives (Schlozman and Tierney, 1986).

LEGISLATIVE ADVOCACY IN ACTION

There are numerous examples of how various groups and organizations have utilized legislative advocacy to effectuate positive changes in their communities. Two of the most noteworthy are the efforts of advocates for mentally retarded persons and advocates for changes in the laws related to drunken driving.

Legislative Advocacy for Mentally Retarded Persons

The development and implementation of federal legislation relating to mentally retarded individuals provides one example of the critical impact that is possible through the efforts of special interest groups. Post-World War II exposés dealing with the treatment of mentally retarded children revealed that institutions

> were housing more and more disabled people with fewer and fewer re-
> sources. Those housed appeared to be more severely retarded than in the
> past.... Needed to fill labor shortages, more capable patients were less likely
> to leave the institution than were their equivalents a generation earlier. In this
> context, brutality, exploitation, neglect, and routinized boredom were too often
> the rule, not the exception.... Americans read that having a retarded child was
> nothing to be ashamed of and that heredity played only a small part. Although
> Americans read that many institutions were snake pits, retarded people in them
> were forgotten children, and neglect had reached the point of euthanasia, they
> also read that placing a child in an institution ... was not a reprehensible thing
> to do (Trent, Jr., 1994: 237–238).

Parents began to form local organizations out of what they believed was a necessity. Public care was often unavailable for their severely retarded children and those children who were kept at home all too often had few resources available to them through the public schools. Media exposés resulted in the closure of the worst of the institutions that housed mentally retarded children. Through the alliance of families, advocates for services for retarded persons, and key legislators, the federal government enacted legislation that ensured additional funding for research into the causes of retardation and the construction of public institutions. Court decisions called for the inclusion of retarded children in public schools and the development of individualized educational programs for each child (Trent, 1994).

Legislative Advocacy against Drunken Driving

The efforts of Mothers Against Drunk Driving (MADD) represents one of the most successful legislative advocacy campaigns to date. MADD was concerned with the numbers of automobile injuries and fatalities that were associated with drunken driving. According to statistics of the National

Highway Traffic Safety Administration, 17,126 persons were killed in alcohol-related accidents in 1996. This constitutes 40.9% of all people killed in traffic accidents that year. If one counts only those deaths in which one or more persons had a blood alcohol content above the legal limit of 0.1% at the time of the accident, the figure of alcohol-related deaths is reduced to 13,395, or approximately 32% of all fatal crashes (Barr, 1996). In comparison, approximately 15% of total road deaths in Great Britain involve accidents in which one or more people have a blood alcohol content (BAC) over the legal limit of .08.

Discussions focusing on the reduction of alcohol-related traffic deaths generally emphasized a reduction in the allowable BAC and a uniform adoption of a minimum drinking age of 21. However, the adoption of 21 as the minimum age has met with some opposition due, in part, to the existence of "blood borders," which allow individuals under the age of 21 to drive into parts of Canada and Mexico, where the drinking age is 18 (Barr, 1996). Levy and Asch of Rutgers University concluded from their study that :

> It does not appear that the high fatality risk presented by new drinkers can be ameliorated by raising the legal drinking age...The problem arises not because we permit people to drink when they are "too young," but rather because we permit them to experience the novelty of "new drinking" at a time when they are legally able to drive. If drinking experience preceded legal driving, a potentially important lifesaving gain may follow (Quoted in Barr, 1996: 279–280).

The National Highway and Traffic Safety Administration has estimated that approximately two-thirds of traffic deaths are associated with aggressive driving. Aggressive driving behavior and the use of cell phones may also be related to vehicular injury (Cellar, Nelson, and Yorke, 2000; Irwin, Fitzgerald, and Berg, 2000). Despite this research, however, the majority of individuals believe that most traffic injuries and fatalities are attributable to drunken driving (Barr, 1996).

The movement against drunken driving, though,

> did not spring from any rise in the incidence or prevalence of drinking-driving or in accidents thought to be related to it. In fact, the rate of road accidents in the United States remains lower than in most other Western industrial democracies. It is widely believed that people who drink and drive end up in accidents in which there is a tragic and costly loss of life, limb, and property. However, none of the organizations or leaders of the movement against drinking-driving have even suggested that their efforts were prompted by some sudden rash of drinking-driving accidents. On the contrary, all claim that their work arose from the fact that the injustices attributed to drinking-driving laws have long been a problem and have never been treated seriously by legislatures and courts (Reinarman, 1988: 91).

MADD came into being as a nonprofit organization in August 1980, largely through the single-minded efforts of Candy Lightner, who had lost her 13-year old daughter as the result of a car accident caused by a drunk driver. At the time of the accident, the driver was on probation for previous DUI (driving under the influence) convictions and had been released on bail, posted by his wife, for another hit-and-run DUI offense that had occurred several days prior to the accident involving Cari Lightner (Reinarman, 1988). The organization was funded with the proceeds from Cari's insurance settlement, Candy Lightner's own savings, and various small grants from the American Council on Alcohol Problems, the National Highway Traffic Safety Administration, and the Levy Foundation (Reinarman, 1988).

From its inception, MADD portrayed itself as the voice of the victim: the individually harmed victim, who survived an accident caused by a drunken driver; the bereaved victim, who has lost a loved one due to the actions of a drunken driver; and the general community activist, who is convinced that community involvement is a key to the resolution of social problems and the restoration of justice (Knoke, 1988; see Weed, 1990).

The 1984 chapter organizing materials of MADD focused on three primary areas of activity: public awareness, legal advocacy, and victim assistance:

> 1. *Public Awareness and Education*: Chapters must educate communities about the seriousness of driving under the influence and to the fact that Americans are individually responsible for their decision to drive while intoxicated.... Community awareness and education includes working with the media (newspapers, television, radio, magazines), Speaker's Bureau programs, poster contests, and annual candlelight vigil and educational programs designed for school-age children and youth. 2. *Legal Advocacy*: Tough laws are effective as a deterrent to driving under the influence, only when these laws are enforced.... MADD members are encouraged to educate criminal justice system personnel and lawmakers of the need for specific types of law, consistent enforcement, and swift and certain punishment of offenders. 3. *Victim Assistance*: As the major goal of MADD is to provide assistance to victims and their families, the chapter must be prepared from the beginning to offer one-on-one support to victims who contact the chapter.... The [MADD] volunteer will make appropriate referrals to appropriate community resources and give the family materials such as the Victim Information Packet and grief brochures.... Volunteers will know enough about the legal process to enable victims to be assertive in knowing their rights through the court case (MADD, 1984: 1–2).

Unlike its competitors, such as the Alliance Against Intoxicated Motorists (AAIM), Boost Alcohol Consciousness Concerning the Health of University Students (BACCHUS), Remove Intoxicated Drivers (RID), and Students Against Driving Drunk (SADD), Mothers Against Drunk Driving accepted funding from the alcohol and broadcasting industries and did not advocate increases in alcohol taxation as a means of reducing alcohol consumption or financing treatment services. Rather, MADD's agenda specifically emphasized individual responsibility, the private moral choice of drinkers, and the resolution of issues through the self-regulation of drinkers, the alcohol industry, the media, and advertisers (Reinarman, 1988). As a result, MADD's efforts received the support of both the alcohol industry and the media:

> Television began this groundswell by giving airtime to MADD's painful [Congressional] testimony.... It did so not merely because of its perceived importance—important but complex and boring testimony is given all the time without a dream of TV coverage—but because it was emotional, sentimental. No sane news director will pass up a grieving, sobbing mother; it is the basic image of tragedy on which TV thrives.... It was the beginning of an orgy of attention. In their search for safe issues on which to take a 10-second position, TV editorial directors pounced on drunk driving as if it were an end-zone fumble. They called repeatedly, almost weekly for "stiffer penalties".... It was heaven-sent: instantly graspable and without opposition.... At the same time, the National Association of Broadcasters organized a massive public service campaign on the problem... Broadcasters aren't stupid; the motivation behind all this attention was forestalling any efforts to ban ads [relating to alcoholic beverages] (Freund, 1985: 1).

MADD'S orientation, with its emphasis on individual responsibility and refusal to address systemic aspects of drunken driving, was in harmony with the policies and rhetoric of the agenda of both Reagan and the New Right. Consequently, the timing of the movement contributed to its success (Marshall and Oleson, 1994; Reinarman, 1988). MADD used its political credibility to achieve major successes in the legislative and law enforcement arenas: the elimination of plea bargaining for drunken driving offenses, the institution of mandatory jail sentences, the reclassification of alcohol-related injuries and death accidents to felonies, the development and implementation of "dram shop" (server) liability laws, the institution of random sobriety checkpoints, and the adoption of mandatory treatment laws and of 21 as the minimum drinking age (Reinarman, 1988).

In order to advance its policy agenda, MADD designed a "Rating the States" (RTS) Program to publicize the efforts of each of the states to combat alcohol-impaired driving. As part of this 1993 program, MADD rated each state in the following areas: gubernatorial leadership, statistics and records, enforcement, administrative and criminal sanctions, regulatory control and availability, legislative efforts, prevention and public awareness efforts, youth issues, self-sufficiency programs, innovative programs, and victim issues. Each state was assigned a grade, ranging from F (the lowest) to A (the highest). Publication of the report often led to renewed efforts by the state to address alcohol-impaired driving (Russell, Voas, Dejong, and Chaloupka, 1995). Several factors have been identified that were critical to the success of this program: (1) the high degree of credibility already associated with MADD as an organization; (2) the high degree of interest that the public generally has in knowing how their own state compares with others; (3) the use of a rating system from A to F that is familiar to almost everyone; (4) a focus on specific political leaders, resulting in political controversy and increased attention and action; and (5) reliance on outside consultants with expertise in marketing and extensive media contacts (Russell, Voas, DeJong, and Chaloupka, 1995).

Other legislative-media efforts did not, however, meet with such resounding success. For instance, in 1991, the Massachusetts legislature was considering the passage of a bill that would have allowed the refusal of an allegedly drunk driver to submit to a breathalyzer test to be used as evidence against him or her in the context of a criminal trial. A particular legislator, however, used parliamentary tactics to prevent the passage of the proposed legislation. MADD used extensive media advocacy efforts to alert the public to the issue. Although the bill was ultimately passed and signed, the actions of MADD led to the public exposure of schisms within the organization, which, in turn, reduced its ultimate effectiveness (DeJong, 1996).

DISCUSSION QUESTIONS

1. Almost one-half of the states have adopted a mechanism known as "ballot initiatives," whereby the voting public can legislate directly by voting on proposed legislation. Californians, for instance, voted on 834 initiatives between 1911 and 1994. Examples of such initiatives include Proposition 13, which limited property tax in California (passed); the Briggs initiative, which would have prohibited gays and lesbians from teaching in public schools (failed); and Proposition 187, which prohibited individuals who were illegally in the United States from receiving many publicly funded services, such as health care and education (passed, but held unconstitutional by the courts). What are the advantages and disadvantages of the initiative procedure, as compared with the usual legislative process?

2. Consider the strategies utilized by MADD to effectuate its goals. To what extent is MADD's success attributable to media advocacy efforts? To legislative advocacy efforts?

REFERENCES

Barr, A. (1996). *Drink: A Social History of America*. New York: Carroll & Graf Publishers, Inc.

Cellar, D.F., Nelson, Z.C., & Yorke, C.M. (2000). The five-factor model and driving behavior: Personality and involvement in vehicular accidents. *Psychological Reports, 86,* 454–456.

Churchill, W. (1947). Speech, Hansard, col. 206. November 11. Quoted in D.L. Faigman. (1999). *Legal Alchemy: The Use and Misuse of Science in Law*. New York: W.H. Freeman.

DeJong, W. (1996). MADD Massachusetts versus Senator Burke: A media advocacy case study. *Health Education Quarterly, 23,* 318–329.

Freund, C.P. (1985). Less filling, tastes great. *City Paper* (Washington, D.C.), Feb. 1–8.

Irwin, M., Fitzgerald, C., & Berg, W.P. (2000). The effect of the intensity of wireless telephone conversations on reaction time in a braking response. *Perceptual and Motor Skills, 90* 1130–1134.

Knoke, D. (1988). Incentives in collective action organizations. *American Sociological Review, 53,* 311–329.

Lautenberg, F. (1993). *Congressional Record,* May 3.

MADD. (1984). *Organizing a Chapter*. Hurst, Texas: Mothers Against Drunk Driving.

Marbury v. Madison. (1803). 5 U.S. 137.

Marshall, M., Oleson, A. (1994). In the pink: MADD and public health policy in the 1990s. *Journal of Public Health Policy, Spring,* 54–68.

Reinarman, C. (1988). The social construction of an alcohol problem: The case of Mothers Against Drunk Drivers and social control in the 1980s. *Theory and Society, 17,* 91–120.

Russell, A., Voas, R.B., DeJong, W., & Chaloupka, M. (1995). MADD rates the states: A media advocacy event to advance the agenda against alcohol-impaired driving. *Public Health Reports, 110,* 240–245.

Schlozman, K.L., & Tierney, J.T. (1986). *Organized Interest and American Democracy*. New York: HarperCollins Publishers, Inc.

Sinclair, B. (1997). *Unorthodox Lawmaking: New Legislative Processes in the U.S. Congress*. Washington, D.C.: Congressional Quarterly, Inc.

Smith, S.S. (1995). *The American Congress*. Boston: Houghton Mifflin.

Trent, J.W., Jr. (1994). *Inventing the Feeble Mind: A History of Mental Retardation in the United States*. Berkeley: University of California Press.

Walker, J.L., Jr. (1991). *Mobilizing Interest Groups in America*. Ann Arbor, MI: University of Michigan Press.

Weed, F.J. (1990). The victim-activist role in the anti-drunk driving movement. *The Sociological Quarterly, 31,* 459–473.

CHAPTER SIX

Promoting Regulatory Change

There is occasions and causes why and wherefore in all things.
William Shakespeare, *Henry V*, V, i, 3

ADMINISTRATIVE AGENCIES

Agency Authority

As indicated in Chapter 5, agencies are responsible for the promulgation of rules. This process occurs at the federal level, the state level and, quite often, the local level. Agencies are created by statutes to carry out tasks that are specified in the statutes that the agencies will implement or enforce. The power that agencies have is delegated to them by the relevant legislature. The legislature cannot delegate its power to an agency. However, a legislature can delegate rulemaking authority to an agency as long as it is the legislature that has decided the underlying policies that will control, and the action of the agency is within the scope of the power that has been delegated to it.

This discussion focuses specifically on the process at the federal level, which is often mirrored in significant ways at the state and local levels.

Oversight of Agency Activities and
Administrative Action

Monitoring Agency Activities

The federal government monitors agency activities in several ways. First, the House of Representatives and the Senate have standing committees that review agency activities in specified areas and sponsor legislation to make needed modifications. Other committees of the government may investigate the conduct of agencies. For instance, Congress has investigated the conduct of the Food and Drug Administration (FDA) with respect to its action, or lack thereof, in regard to the use of silicone breast implants. The Administrative Conference of the United States is responsible for the analysis of federal administrative agencies and administrative law and may advise Congress with regard to recommended modifications. Ombudsmen are utilized by some federal agencies to investigate public complaints about specified administrative action and to recommend corrections where appropriate. Finally, legislators may intervene in administrative matters involving their constituents.

Despite these mechanisms that permit Congress to have some degree of control over agency action, that control is not unlimited. For instance, Congress does not have the power to appoint the members of the agency engaged in rulemaking or adjudication. Second, Congress may not remove officials engaged in executive functions.

The executive branch of the government also maintains some control over agency action. First, the President of the United States has the power to appoint the heads of the federal administrative agencies, subject to the approval of the Senate. The President, by statute, has the power to create, abolish, and reorganize agencies within the federal branch of government.

Monitoring Agency Rulemaking

Controls on agency rulemaking activities exist through the judiciary, the legislature, and the executive branch of government. The courts may review the rules to ensure that they are within the scope of authority granted to the agency by the relevant statute and that the agency has followed the mandated procedures in promulgating the rules. The legislature retains oversight responsibility and authority, as well as budgetary authority. The executive branch of government has input on rulemaking through communications with agency staff and/or may require that an agency contemplating certain types of action follow specified procedures. For instance, the National Environmental Policy Act requires that agencies engaging in rulemaking make an environmental assessment of their proposed action and consider alternatives that would be less damaging to the environment.

Agency Development of Rules

The Rulemaking Process

Agencies may engage in both formal and informal rulemaking. Formal rulemaking involves an adjudicatory procedure, whereby a hearing must be conducted on the record in order to adopt a rule. If formal rulemaking is required, this will be specified in the relevant statute. Formal rulemaking is very inefficient and, consequently, is not utilized very often.

Informal rulemaking is governed by the specified provisions of the Administrative Procedure Act. In order for these provisions to apply, however, the object of the debate or discussion must be a rule within the meaning of the Administrative Procedure Act. The term "rule" is synonymous with the term "regulation."

The Administrative Procedure Act defines a rule as "the whole or part of an agency statement of general or particular applicability and future effect designed to implement, interpret, or prescribe law or policy" (5 U.S.C. § 551). There are, according to this definition, several critical elements: (1) the rule applies to situations that will arise in the future and (2) in general, the rule applies to a class of people or entities. The agencies that promulgate rules have the power to do so because Congress has authorized or directed that they promulgate rules pursuant to specific statutes. These rules must be consistent with both the statute that has authorized their promulgation and the Constitution. As indicated by the definition of rules, rules may simply implement the provisions of a particular statute, they may interpret terms and provisions that are contained in the statute, or they may operationalize (prescribe) how a goal that was stated in the governing statute is to be effectuated. For instance, the Occupational Safety and Health Act seeks "to assure so far as possible every working man and woman in the Nation safe and healthy work conditions" (29 U.S.C § 553). It is up to the Occupational Safety and Health Administration (OSHA) to define what is meant by "safe" and "health."

Although rulemaking had become a critical government function by the late 1930s, the process by and extent to which rules were formulated varied across different government agencies (Kerwin, 1999). The extent to which agency decisions could or would deviate from these rules, once they had been formulated, also differed by agency. Notice of the rules that governed a particular situation was similarly variable because, at the time, there was no single mechanism for the publication, indexing, and dissemination of relevant rules. The Administrative Procedure Act, enacted in 1946, attempts to address some of these inconsistencies by requiring that notice of a proposed rule be provided to afford interested persons an opportunity to comment on its various aspects prior to the rule's finalization, adoption, and implementation. The text of the relevant statutory provision (5 United States Code section 553) is set forth below.

(a) This section applies, according to the provisions thereof, except to the extent that there is involved—

(1) a military or foreign affairs function of the United States; or

(2) a matter relating to agency management or personnel or to public property, loans, grants, benefits, or contracts.

(b) General notice of proposed rule making shall be published in the Federal Register, unless persons subject thereto are named and either personally served or otherwise have actual notice thereof in accordance with law. The notice shall include—

(1) a statement of the time, place, and nature of public rule making proceedings;

(2) reference to the legal authority under which the rule is proposed; and

(3) either the terms or substance of the proposed rule or a description of the subjects and issues involved.

Except when notice or hearing is required by statute, this subsection does not apply—

(A) to interpretive rules, general statements of policy, or rules of agency organization, procedure, or practice; or

(B) when the agency for good cause finds (and incorporates the finding and a brief statement of reasons therefore in the rules issued) that notice and public procedure thereon are impracticable, unnecessary, or contrary to the public interest.

(c) After notice required by this section, the agency shall give interested persons an opportunity to participate in the rule making through submission of written data, views, or arguments with or without opportunity for oral presentation After consideration of the relevant material presented, the agency shall incorporate in the rules adopted a concise general statement of their basis and purpose. When rules are required to be made on the record after opportunity for an agency hearing, sections 556 and 557 of this title shall apply instead of this subsection.

(d) The required publication or service of a substantive rule shall be made not less than 30 days before its effective date, except—

(1) a substantive rule which grants or recognizes an exemption or relieves a restriction;

(2) interpretive rules and statements of policy;

(3) as otherwise provided by the agency for good cause found and published with the rule.

(e) Each agency shall give an interested person the right to petition for the issuance, amendment, or repeal of a rule.

Figure 6.1.   Relevant Statutory Provision of the Administrative Procedure Act (1946).

The critical elements of the notice and comment procedure include (1) a statement of the time, place, and nature of the public rulemaking proceedings; (2) reference to the legal authority under which the rule is being proposed; and (3) the terms or content of the proposed rule or a description of the subjects and issues to be addressed. As part of this procedure, the agency must publish or make available any critical data so that individuals who wish to comment on a rule can do so in a way that is meaningful.

There is no provision that specifies how much notice the public must be given for the public to submit comments to a proposed rule. However, once the final rule is published by the agency, a minimum period of 30 days must elapse before the final rule can become effective.

After the agency receives the public comments, it must actually consider those comments. In issuing the subsequent rule, the agency is required to prepare a statement that explains its reasoning for adopting the rule as it has. This statement must respond to the public comments that were received and explains which of the suggestions were and were not followed and why or why not. The statutory section establishing this procedure is set forth below.

The comments that are submitted in response to a proposed rule are generally part of the public file. Ex parte contacts, meaning those that are off-the-record, are permitted in the context of rulemaking. Some specific agencies require that all written and oral ex parte communications with the rulemakers be disclosed during the rulemaking process. There is no prohibition on attempts by the legislature or the executive branch to influence the rulemakers through ex parte communications. For instance, meetings between the President of the United States and an agency are considered to be appropriate because the President is constitutionally responsible for all executive decisions (*Sierra Club v. Costle*, 1981). It is true that a rulemaker may be biased in making rules, but there is no prohibition against this and the rulemaker is not required to be disqualified because rulemaking is intended to be a political process. A rulemaker will only be disqualified for bias if there is a clear and convincing showing that he or she is unwilling to consider fairly issues that are critical to the disposition of the rulemaking .

Some agencies have experimented in a procedure known as negotiated rulemaking. In this procedure, individuals representing all affected interests are called together by the agency in order to try to reach a consensus on the relevant issues. The rule that these individuals agree on is then the rule that is the subject of the notice and comment procedure, outlined above. Negotiated rulemaking may be most successful where there is a limited number of identifiable interests and individuals can be identified to represent those interests. An agency wishing to avail itself of negotiated rulemaking procedures must publish a notice indicating such in the *Federal*

Register. That notice must include a list of proposed committee members and a proposed agenda and timetable.

The *Code of Federal Regulations* (CFR) was begun in 1938, in an effort to provide a single authoritative compilation of the rules promulgated by federal agencies. The CFR is organized by titles, which correspond to the analogous titles of the United States Code, containing the statutory provisions governing those particular rules. For instance, title 8 of the United States Code contains the statutory provisions governing the admission of noncitizens into the United States, including provisions that specify health grounds for which individuals can be excluded. The corresponding regulations are contained in titles 8 and 42 of the *Code of Federal Regulations*. These rules delineate what specific diseases constitute a basis of exclusion and how, when, and where the medical examination is to be conducted to determine if an individual seeking entry into the United States is afflicted with one of the conditions for which he or she can be excluded.

Specific titles of the *Code of Federal Regulations*, though, are republished only every one or two years. However, revisions to existing regulations, or rules, are made much more frequently. Too, Congress may pass legislation that mandates that an agency promulgate relevant regulations but the number of rules that must be developed is so massive that it can only be accomplished through a gradual, incremental process. As an example, the Environmental Protection Agency estimated that the passage of the Clean Air Act of 1990 required that it develop and implement approximately 300 to 400 new rules (Kerwin, 1999). Accordingly, new and revised rules are first published in the *Federal Register*, which is published on an almost daily basis.

Types of Rules

The statutory provision above refers to various types of rules, such as interpretive rules and substantive rules. Rules are often classified according to the function that they serve. "Legislative" or "substantive" rules are formulated by an agency, pursuant to a congressional mandate or authorization. Such rules, once formulated and implemented, require that the agency adhere to the procedures and standards specified by the rules. These rules can only be promulgated and implemented through the notice and comment procedure. "Interpretive" rules are utilized to explain existing law and policy. Unlike legislative rules, they do not impose new legal obligations but, instead, explain how the agency is interpreting its legal obligation pursuant to specific legislation. Interpretive rules are considered to be advisory in nature and, although they are often published in the *Federal Register*, they are not subject to the notice and comment procedure described in the statutory provision above. "Procedural" rules define an organization and the processes that it utilizes.

Rules are generally prospective in nature. This is particularly true of legislative rules. Interpretive rules may be retroactive in nature if Congress has expressly granted authority to the agency to promulgate rules that will have an effect retroactively.

Additionally, agencies may promulgate regulations that provide for criminal sanctions. However, they may not prosecute or imprison for the violation of those regulations. Only courts may order imprisonment as a punishment for the violation of a regulation. Civil penalties can be imposed, but punitive damages may not be.

Exceptions to Informal Rulemaking Requirements

Several exceptions to the requirement of notice and comment exist. These include categorical exceptions, procedure exceptions, and good cause exceptions. In addition, interpretive rules and policy statements are not subject to the notice and comment provisions.

Categorical Exceptions. Military and foreign affairs are not subject to the notice and comment provisions of the Administrative Procedure Act. Matters relating to agency management or personnel or to public property are similarly not subject to these provisions.

Procedure Exception. The Administrative Procedure Act provides that rules "of agency organization, procedure, or practice" are exempt from the notice and comment requirement. They are also exempt from the delayed effective date requirement, which provides that a period of at least 30 days must elapse from the publication of the rule to the date it becomes effective.

Good Cause Exception. The agency will be excused from complying with the notice and comment procedure "when the agency for good cause finds (and incorporates the finding and a brief statement of reasons therefore in the rules issued) that notice and public procedure thereon are impracticable, unnecessary, or contrary to the public interest" (5 U.S.C. § 553(b)(B)). "Unnecessary" means that the regulation has only a trivial impact or that it will relieve regulated parties of a regulatory burden. Notice and comment will be found to be contrary to the public interest or impracticable when immediate action is required and the delay caused by the notice and comment procedure would either harm the public safety or thwart the underlying legislative intent (*Union of Concerned Scientists v. Nuclear Regulatory Commission*, 1983).

Interpretive Rules. As indicated previously, interpretive rules are those which attempt to explain the meaning of particular terms in a statute or a previous rule. It may be difficult, however, to decide which rules are interpretive and which are legislative. In making this distinction, the courts will often focus on the intention of the agency in promulgating the rule. A rule is legislative if the agency had the power to make legislative rules and intended to use it. However, if an agency did not have such power or if it had it but did not intend to use it, the rule will be considered to be interpretive. The courts will give great weight in making this determination to how the agency initially characterized the rule. If, however, the rule compels specified behavior, a court may find that it is legislative in nature even if the agency characterized it as interpretive (*Chamber of Commerce v. OSHA*, 1980).

Policy Statements. A policy statement sets forth how an agency intends to perform a discretionary function, such as future prosecutions, investigations, or adjudications. The notice and comment provision and the delayed effective date provision do not apply with respect to policy statements.

It may be difficult to distinguish a policy statement from agency pronouncements of a different nature. A pronouncement will be found to be a policy statement if it is tentative. This means that it may inform the public and the staff of the agency how the agency will exercise its discretion, but it is not definitive. If the pronouncement is definitive, the statement will be considered to be a legislative rule, subject to the notice and comment provision.

Challenging Agency Rules

It is not uncommon that agency rules will be challenged in court. The record that will go before the court includes the proposed rule, the notice of the proposed rulemaking, the public comments that were received, the transcript of any public hearings, and the agency's statement of basis and purpose. In general, the courts will consider as part of the record only the materials that were before the agency at the time that it made the decision regarding the rule (*Camp v. Pitts*, 1973). However, if the court needs assistance in understanding the technical material that is contained in the record, the court may permit the introduction of expert testimony to assist it (*Bunker Hill Co. v. Environmental Protection Agency*, 1977). The assessment of who can challenge an agency rule and under what circumstances is quite technical and will not be reviewed here.

Agency Action in the Face of Uncertainty

Many federal agencies are concerned with the regulation of substances that are potentially harmful. For instance, the Environmental Protection Agency (EPA) is charged with the responsibility of regulating pesticide residues on raw agricultural products, the quality of drinking water, the quality of air, and synthetic waste materials. The Food and Drug Administration (FDA) is responsible for overseeing issues related to food additives, cosmetics, drugs, and medical devices. The Occupational Safety and Health Administration (OSHA) regulates workplace exposures to chemicals and establishes and enforces occupational health and safety standards.

Not infrequently, multiple agencies may have authority to regulate the use of the same substance, albeit in different situations or contexts. For instance, the Occupational Safety and Health Administration, pursuant to the Occupational Safety and Health Act of 1970, regulated exposure to vinyl chloride in factories. The Environmental Protection Agency also regulated vinyl chloride emissions from factories, but under the aegis of the Clean Air Act. Vinyl chloride in household aerosols was regulated by the Consumer Product Safety Commission pursuant to the Federal Hazardous Substances Act, while the Food and Drug Administration regulated both cosmetic aerosols containing vinyl chloride (through the Food, Drug, and Cosmetic Act), and drug aerosols (through the New Drug Amendments of 1962) (Doniger, 1978). Numerous agencies have shared responsibility for the control of exposure to lead: the Environmental Protection Agency for airborne emissions from autos and industry; the Occupational Safety and Health Administration for manufacturing and industrial processes; the Environmental Protection Agency for industrial wastes and their disposal in rivers and lakes; the Food and Drug Administration for lead contained in pottery and food; and the National Institutes of Health, in addition to various other agencies, for health effects research relating to lead (Billick, 1981).

The rules that agencies formulate to address the potential threats that are posed by exposures to potentially harmful substances must be based on information. The statute that gives the agency authority to promulgate rules will often define the kinds of information that the agency may utilize during this process. For instance, the Occupational Safety and Health Act provides that OSHA's development of standards

> shall be based on research, demonstrations, experiments and such other information as may be appropriate. In addition to the attainment of the highest degree of health and safety protection for the employee other considerations shall be the latest available scientific data in the field, the feasibility of the standards and the experience gained under this and other health and safety laws (29 United States Code section 655(b)(5)).

Setting Standards

Some statutes require that, in setting standards, agencies consider only health concerns in formulating standards, while other statutory provisions mandate that an agency consider economic, as well as health, issues (Doniger, 1978). Sometimes, an agency is responsible for regulating potential exposures under several statutes, each of which mandates the application of a different standard. For instance, the EPA is required by the Safe Drinking Water Act to establish "maximum contaminant levels [at which] no known or anticipated adverse effects" could occur, while still allowing an "adequate margin of safety." In contrast, the Federal Insecticide, Fungicide, and Rodenticide Act (FIFRA) requires that the EPA set standards that will prevent "unreasonable adverse effect" while considering "the economic, social, and environmental costs and benefits" (Environmental Protection Agency, 1988).

INFLUENCING AGENCY RULEMAKING

As in the legislative process, organizations and individuals can act as advocates in the rulemaking process. First, they can review relevant regulations proposed in the Federal *Register* and influence the formulation of the final regulation by responding during the statutory notice and comment period to the initial regulation. Second, they can approach an agency directly to request that the agency promulgate proposed regulations that address a particular concern. Or, advocates can draft proposed regulations themselves and then submit them to the appropriate agency and request that the agency review these regulations, modify them as appropriate, and then publish them for notice and comment.

Regulatory Change and Tobacco Control

One of the best examples of how advocates can effectuate regulatory change is provided by Maryland's statewide coalition for the control of tobacco.

As recently as 1993, Maryland had no organized agenda for the control of tobacco (Wasserman, 1997), although Maryland was known as a state with one of the highest rates of cancer and the Maryland Cancer Consortium (1991) had identified tobacco use as the primary risk factor for cancer mortality in Maryland. The Local Health Officers' Association, comprised of health officers from each county in Maryland and the city of Baltimore, resolved in July 1993 to advocate for increased tobacco control, through such measures as the prohibition of tobacco sales to minors, a tax increase on tobacco products, and the imposition of a smoking ban in public areas. The Association developed a multi-target strategy: legislation, media and marketing, grassroots community, and regulatory action (Wasserman, 1997).

In part through the efforts of the Association, and in response to the deaths of three school maintenance workers resulting from an explosion caused by a lit cigarette, the Maryland Occupational Health and Safety Board in 1994 issued regulations that banned smoking in the workplace, including bars and restaurants. The regulations were later modified in 1995 to exclude bars and the bar areas of restaurants, in response to concerns expressed by the legislature (Wasserman, 1997).

DISCUSSION QUESTIONS

1. There is a lack of parity in health insurance policies' coverage of treatment for mental illness as compared with treatment for illness deemed to be physical. Assume that as a public health professional, you wish to advocate for parity in coverage. How could legislative or regulatory advocacy be utilized to bring about parity? Would legislative or regulatory advocacy be more effective on a long-term basis?

2. Consider the action of the Food and Drug Administration with respect to silicone breast implants. The FDA is authorized to regulate medical devices pursuant to the Federal Food, Drug, and Cosmetics Act of 1938, which seeks to "prohibit the movement of interstate commerce of adulterated or misbranded food, drugs, devices and cosmetics." Silicone breast implants were "grandfathered" in, enabling the manufacturers to continue marketing the devices without offering proof of safety and effectiveness. Initially, manufacturers and plastic surgeons argued that the implants were safe for use and the FDA did not require proof of this assertion. By 1970, however, some scientists had raised concerns regarding the safety of the silicone implants. Later, as a result of new information, the FDA on January 6, 1992 issued a voluntary moratorium that urged surgeons to refrain from using silicone gel implants and manufacturers from supplying them. In April of that same year, then-commissioner of the FDA, David Kessler, announced that the availability of silicone breast

implants would be restricted to clinical trials. Is this an example of regulatory advocacy? Why or why not? What factors contributed to the FDA's actions?

REFERENCES

Administrative Procedure Act, 5 U.S.C. §§ 551, 553.

Billick, I.H. (1981). Lead: A case study in interagency policy-making. *Environmental Health Perspectives, 42*, 73–79.

Bunker Hill Co. v. Environmental Protection Agency. (1973). 572 F.2d 1286 (9th Cir.).

Camp v. Pitts. (1973). 411 U.S. 138.

*Chamber of Commerce v. OSHA,*636 f.2D 464 (D.C. Cir. 1980).

Doniger, D.D. (1978). *The Law and Policy of Toxic Substances Control: A Case Study of Vinyl Chloride.* Baltimore: Johns Hopkins University Press.

Environmental Protection Agency. (1988). *Regulation Development in EPA.* Washington, D.C.: Author.

Kerwin, C.M. (1999). *Rulemaking: How Government Agencies Write Law and Make Policy.* Washington, D.C.: Congressional Quarterly, Inc.

Maryland Cancer Consortium. (1991). *Maryland Cancer Control Plan.* Cited in M.P. Wasserman (1997). Building a statewide coalition for tobacco control, 1993-present. *Journal of Public Health Management Practice, 3*, 8–13.

Sierra Club v. Costle. (1981). 657 F.2d 298 (D.C. Cir.).

Union of Concerned Scientists v. Nuclear Regulatory Commission. (1983). 711 F.2d 370 (D.C. Cir.).

Wasserman, M.P. (1997). Building a statewide coalition for tobacco control, 1993-present. *Journal of Public Health Management Practice, 3*, 8–13.

5 U.S.C. §§ 551, 553.

29 U.S.C. §§ 553, 655.

CHAPTER SEVEN

Using the Courts

In a society such as ours, but basically in any society, there are manifold relations of power which permeate, characterize and constitute the social body, and these relations of power cannot themselves be established, consolidated nor implemented without the production, accumulation, circulation, and functioning of a discourse. There can be no possible exercise of power without a certain economy of discourses of truth which operates through and on the basis of this association. We are subject to the production of truth through power and we cannot exercise power except through the production of truth
(Foucault, 1979: 93).

THE STRUCTURE OF THE COURT SYSTEM

The state and federal court systems can be thought of as pyramids. At the very base of the pyramid are the lowest courts. At the mid-level of the pyramid sit the courts of first appeal and, at the pinnacle of the pyramid, sits the supreme court of the state or of the federal court system. Different states, however, name these various levels differently. For instance, the supreme court in California is known as the Supreme Court, but in Massachusetts it is known as the Massachusetts Supreme Judicial Court, and in New York it is called the Court of Appeals.

In the state court system, the lowest level courts are often divided into those that have limited jurisdiction and those that have general jurisdiction. Those with limited jurisdiction often hear cases involving less serious offenses and civil lawsuits that do not involve large sums of money. Courts of general jurisdiction may hear cases involving monetary sums over a specified amount or more serious matters. Courts of general jurisdiction are often divided into special courts due to the volume of cases and the need for specialized expertise. Examples of such specialized courts include juvenile court, family court, and traffic court.

The mid-level courts, or appellate courts, have the power to hear appeals from the decisions of the lower courts. This is known as appellate jurisdiction, as contrasted with original jurisdiction, which is the power to hear a case at its inception. The appellate courts may have original jurisdiction with respect to a limited range of cases. The state supreme court may hear appeals from the appellate courts.

The lowest tier on this pyramid in the federal system consists of the federal district courts. These courts hear cases involving crimes that arise under federal statutes, such as making false statements on a federal application. They have jurisdiction over cases in which the citizen of one state is suing a citizen of another state (diversity of citizenship case) if the amount in dispute is greater than a specified minimum. (State courts may also hear cases in which a citizen of one state is suing a citizen of another state. This is known as concurrent jurisdiction. Not infrequently, the party who did not file the original lawsuit may ask to have the case removed to federal court.) The federal district courts may also hear cases arising under the federal constitution and cases arising under federal statutes.

Appeals from the decisions of the district courts are made to the federal Court of Appeal having jurisdiction over the circuit in which the district court sits. Twelve of these Circuit Courts are for named circuits, one is for cases arising in the District of Columbia, and one is for the Federal Circuit, which has jurisdiction over claims that are exclusively within the domain of federal law, patent and trademark law.

The Supreme Court hears appeals from the Courts of Appeal. However, in most situations, there is no automatic right to appeal to the Supreme Court. Rather, the Supreme Court chooses the cases that it will hear. Request to have an appeal heard is made through a *writ of certiorari*, which is a petition to file an appeal.

Apart from the judicial system, some agencies may have the power to resolve cases administratively. For instance, the Office of Research Integrity has the authority to investigate and adjudicate allegations of scientific misconduct. Appeals proceed to the Department Appeals Board and, from there, to court if necessary.

THE LAWSUIT AS ADVOCACY

Bringing a Lawsuit: The Strategy

The use of the lawsuit as a form of advocacy has been recommended (1) as one component of a multi-faceted strategy for change, such as efforts to end discrimination against individuals infected with HIV; (2) in situations where the delay resulting from a lawsuit may itself constitute success, such as the delay in the construction of a development in an environmentally protected area; (3) in situations in which it is not possible to prevail politically, such as efforts to end environmental injustice; and (4) in situations where the litigation itself may effectuate change, even if a specific lawsuit is ultimately lost, such as lawsuits to end police delays and inaction in responding to domestic violence calls (see Shaw, 2001).

Because of the complexity of the litigation process, as discussed below, lawyers are often involved in advocacy efforts through the courts. Community-based activists may fear or resent this involvement, believing that influence will be transferred to the attorneys and away from social change activists involved in the particular issue (Shaw, 2001). Several tactics have been identified, however, that may help community activists retain their power and influence, even during the litigation process. First, the services of attorneys may be retained for technical assistance only. In such situations, the attorney's role is limited to providing information and to representing individuals or the group, but does not include the ability to decide the future course of action. Second, decisions relating to nonlegal matters should be made in the presence of community leaders. Third, meetings should be held at a familiar site, rather than a law office, to reduce the possibility that those in attendance will be intimidated by surroundings that are both unfamiliar and quite formal. Fourth, community activists can choose to work with attorneys who understand their concerns and are willing to work within the prescribed parameters (Shaw, 2001).

Bringing a Civil Lawsuit: The Procedure

The court system can be used by individuals and organizations to advocate for change. A civil lawsuit is commenced through the filing of a complaint by a party to the lawsuit. The complaint must, in general, state the nature of the claim, the facts to support the claim, and the amount in controversy. The defendant will be served with a copy of the complaint, together with a summons. The summons indicates that the defendant must respond to the complaint in some fashion within a specified period of time or the plaintiff will win the lawsuit by default.

The defendant will then answer the complaint, and will admit, deny, or plead ignorance to each allegation of the complaint. The defendant may also file a countersuit against the plaintiff or against a third party. The defendant may also ask that the court dismiss the plaintiff's action, claiming that the court has no jurisdiction to entertain the case or that the plaintiff failed to state a cause of action.

Following the initiation of the lawsuit and the answer by the defendant, there will be a period of discovery, during which each party to the action will have the opportunity to gather additional facts to support its case, to identify expert witnesses that the other side may call, and to identify weaknesses in the opposing party's case. Discovery may include depositions, written interrogatories, the production of documents, a request for a mental or physical examination, and a request for admissions. Those that are most relevant to the health research context are depositions, written interrogatories, a request for the production of documents, and a request for admissions.

The trial itself consists of numerous stages:

1. the opening statement of the plaintiff,
2. the opening statement of the defendant,
3. the presentation of direct evidence by the plaintiff, with cross-examination of each witness by the defendant, re-direct by the plaintiff, and re-cross by the defendant,
4. the presentation of direct evidence by the defendant, with cross-examination by the plaintiff, re-direct by the defendant, and re-cross by the plaintiff,
5. presentation of rebuttal evidence by the plaintiff,
6. presentation of rebuttal evidence by the defendant,
7. plaintiff's argument to the jury,
8. defendant's argument to the jury,
9. plaintiff's closing argument to the jury,
10. defendant's closing argument to the jury,
11. instructions from the judge to the jury, and
12. jury deliberation and verdict.

Some lawsuits are brought by large groups of persons acting together as a class; such lawsuits are known as class actions. In order to bring a class action, the class must be so numerous that joining the individual members together in a lawsuit is impractical, the action involves questions of law or fact that are common to all of the members of the class, the claims or defenses of the named individual(s) maintaining the lawsuit are typical of all of the class members, and the person representing the class is able to protect the interests of all of the members of the class (Federal Rule of Civil Procedure 23).

The type of remedy that may be available to a plaintiff or plaintiffs in a lawsuit will depend on the basis on which the suit is brought. An individual suing to rectify the unlawful termination of his or her employment due to discrimination may seek reinstatement of his or her employment, monetary damages to compensate for the legal expenditures related to bringing the lawsuit and the loss of income, and/or monetary damages to punish the offending party. Individuals or groups suing to stop a development that is threatening the public's health would be likely to request injunctive and declaratory relief, meaning that the court would order a halt to the project and declare that the process of the development has not followed the proper procedure set forth by law.

ADVOCACY IN THE COURTS: CASE STUDIES

Lawsuits and Community Action: A Multi-Faceted Approach to End AIDS Discrimination

Background

The first cases of the disease that would eventually come to be known as AIDS appeared in 1981, in a number of otherwise healthy gay men. Major media networks emphasized the existence of a new "gay plague," although subsequent reports focused on the transmission of the disease beyond the borders of this population, to "needle-using drug addicts" and Haitians and to the "innocent victims," the hemophiliacs, the children, and the recipients of blood transfusions (Cook and Colby, 1992). Even as we learned more about the biological basis of the disease (Oppenheimer, 1992), we defined it primarily as a sexually transmitted disease, rather than as a virus. AIDS, then, was seen as a disease occurring among those who violated the accepted moral order, the link between those who were socially deviant and those who were morally correct. One journalist wrote, "Suddenly a lot of people fear that they and their families might suddenly catch some mysterious, fatal illness which until now has been confined to society's social outcasts" (Brandt, 1988: 155). Fear itself became epidemic:

> Fighting the fear of AIDS, it seems is as important as fighting the disease itself.... As researchers attempt to conquer this disease called AIDS, public officials attempt to conquer the epidemic of fear.... It is a delicate balancing act, raising the level of concern for the disease on the one hand, while reducing the level of panic on the other (ABC, June 20, 1983, quoted in Cook and Colby, 1992: 90).

News stories portrayed the extent of the fear: police officers wearing gloves, television technicians refusing to fit a microphone on a person with AIDS, refusals to admit persons with AIDS into nursing homes, the inability of agencies to locate foster homes for children of AIDS-afflicted mothers, the increased violence against gay men, and the loss of private insurance coverage and/or employment by individuals diagnosed with AIDS (Cook and Colby, 1992). Calls were made for the quarantine of those with AIDS (Musto, 1988). Discrimination assumed not only these forms, but also more subtle forms, such as the refusal or failure of state and federal governments to acknowledge the existence of HIV/AIDS and to make provisions for the transmission of the disease and the care of those who were already infected. Ultimately, the Presidential Commission on Human Immunodeficiency Virus Epidemic concluded that discrimination was significantly hindering the country's ability to limit HIV transmission.

Advocates utilized numerous approaches in their efforts to combat discrimination against those who were—and are—infected with HIV/AIDS. The organization known as ACT UP was created in March 1987 specifically to organize direct action, such as marches, rallies, and other forms of public protest, in order to instigate and ensure an adequate governmental response to the HIV/AIDS epidemic. The need for direct action was premised on then-existing circumstances. First, homophobia seemed to be a cornerstone of the Republican platform, and anti-gay groups had supported Reagan during his bid for the presidency. Not only did Reagan himself fail to mention AIDS until 1985, but many in his administration appeared to view AIDS as a punishment from God for immoral behavior, such as homosexuality and sex outside of marriage (Shaw, 2001). Second, AIDS emerged during the Reagan presidency, an administration that was committed to a reduction in domestic spending for purposes other than the national defense. The administration, then, was not inclined to increase spending for HIV prevention and care. Third, the medical, scientific, and pharmaceutical establishments were seen as indifferent to the need of HIV-infected individuals to obtain experimental drugs to treat the disease, as there was clearly no cure available (Shaw, 2001; Shilts, 1987). The creation of ACT UP

> reflected a growing consensus in the gay community that politely accepting government, scientific, and corporate inaction was equivalent to accepting death sentences for thousands of people infected with or already suffering from AIDS. The consequences of continuing to work patiently through "the system" could not be more stark. People were dying, and the health care delivery system was unconcerned about their fate. Six gay men created the motto "Silence=Death," put it on a pink triangle against a black background, and posted the message at their own expense (Shaw, 201: 215).

Efforts to end discrimination against those who were HIV-infected were also instituted through "the system," often on an individual basis to address a specific situation. Existing legislation provided the basis for much of the litigation brought in this context. And, although the litigation may have been brought in response to a specific individual's situation, the resolution of such situation under federal law provided the basis for the resolution of subsequent, similar situations.

As an example, the Americans with Disabilities Act (ADA), enacted in 1990, seeks to prohibit discrimination against qualified individuals as a result of their disabilities. "Disability" includes a wide range of both physical and mental disabilities that "substantially limit one or more of the major life activities of that individual; a record of such impairment; or being regarded as having such an impairment." In order to be qualified, the disabled person must meet all of the performance criteria for the specific job, service, or benefit. Concomitantly, there is an obligation on the part of the employer or provider to "reasonably accommodate" the disabled individual to allow him or her to meet those criteria. Lawsuits have also been premised on the federal Rehabilitation Act of 1973. Unlike the ADA, the legislation provides protection for federal employees.

Lawsuits have been brought by parents of HIV-infected children against school districts that placed HIV-infected children alone in a separate modular classroom (*Robertson v. Granite City Community Unit School District*, 1988) or in a glass booth (*Martinez v. School Board of Hillsborough County, Florida*, 1989) and that excluded HIV-infected children from ordinary schools (*Doe v. Dolton Elementary School District No. 148*, 1988; *Doe v. Belleville School District, No. 118*, 1987; *Ray v. School District of DeSoto County*, 1987; *Phipps v. Saddleback Valley Unified School District*, 1988). In the employment arena, lawsuits have been filed to challenge the termination of employment without a hearing (*Raytheon v. Fair Employment and Housing Commission, Estate of Chadbourne*, 1989; *Shuttleworth v. Broward County*, 1986), and demotions based on having HIV (*Chalk v. U.S.*, 1988). The courts have held that HIV infection does not justify unfair treatment by employers (*Raytheon v. Fair Employment and Housing Commission, Estate of Chadbourne*, 1989; *Chalk v. U.S.*, 1988; *Shuttleworth v. Broward County*, 1986). Lawsuits have also been filed for discrimination in housing (*Seitzman v. Hudson River Association*, 1987) and for the refusal of health care professionals to treat someone with HIV infection (*Doe v. Centinela Hospital*, 1988; *Hurwitz v. New York City Commission on Human Rights*, 1988).

Direct community action may include circulating petitions, holding demonstrations and marches, rating political candidates and agencies, picketing shareholders' meetings, staging sit-ins, and soliciting media coverage (Brown and Mikkelsen, 1997; Austin and Schill, 1994).

Delay Equals Success: Lawsuits

Litigation for the purpose of delay has been used most frequently in the environmental arena where, for instance, health advocates may want to halt a development project that threatens a community with adverse health effects due to increased pollution, overcrowding, or hazardous traffic patterns. Lawsuits in this context have been used to challenge the construction of high-rise office buildings in major cities and the encroachment of new housing developments on agricultural land and open space.

Litigation in this context is often brought under a particular statute that requires that an environmental impact report assess the impact of the proposed project on the environment prior to commencement of the project. Advocates may claim that the environmental impact was inadequately addressed during the planning review process, requiring the development of a new report approved by the local planning agency, which is then also subject to challenge. The delay resulting from the litigation may itself trigger the termination of the project due to time-sensitive financing opportunities for the developer, changes in the development's company's priorities or structure during the period of delay, a deterioration in the overall economic climate, an increase in interest rates, and/or escalating legal costs to defend the project (Shaw, 2001).

The California Environmental Quality Act (CEQA), for instance, emphasizes the state's intent to take "steps to identify any critical thresholds for the health and safety of the people of the state and take all coordinated actions necessary to prevent such thresholds being reached" (California Public Resources Code, 1996: section 21000(d)). In order to effectuate this goal, governmental agencies must consider the qualitative factors, economic factors, technical factors, short- and long-term costs and benefits, and existing alternatives to proposed actions that affect the environment. Accordingly, public agencies that propose a project that will affect the environment must prepare an environmental impact report to "identify the significant effects on the environment of a project, and to indicate the manner in which those significant effects can be mitigated or avoided" (California Public Resources Code, 1996: section 21002.1(a)). Public review and comment is an essential element of CEQA proceedings (*Dixon v. Superior Court*, 1994). In one instance, advocates filed a complaint under CEQA for injunctive and declaratory relief, claiming that the construction of a kiln for burning scrap tires would release toxic chemicals into the air, potentially resulting in adverse health effects to the public. A portion of that complaint appears below.

1.   The region is heavily polluted. It contains twenty-four toxic sites identified by the California Environmental Protection Agency (CEPA), Department of Toxic Substance Control, with eight in

[OurTown] alone. Extremely high levels ... of dioxin contaminate one site. The only state facility that burns commercial hazardous waste is located within twenty miles of Respondent. In [YourTown], twelve miles south of [OurTown], the childhood cancer rate between the years of 1975 and 1984 has been found to be six times greater than the rate in other areas of California.

2.   Respondent operates a kiln at [address], approximately twelve miles south of [OurTown].

3.   On March 24, 1994, Respondent, which currently uses coal as its only fuel, submitted a plan to the Air District to modify its facility to burn whole scrap tires for up to 20 percent of its fuel needs (hereafter called "Project.")

4.   Burning whole scrap tires in cement kilns creates an array of toxic byproducts, including dioxins (polychlorinated dibenzodioxins), furans (polychlorinated dibenzofurans), polyaromatic hydrocarbons (PAHs), polychlorinated iphenols (PCBs), hexavelent chromium, and cadmium. These chemicals have been identified by the State of California ... as causing cancer or reproductive toxicity.

5.   Despite oral and written comments requesting CEQA review process for the Project to review the health and environmental dangers it might cause, including requests for a factsheet on the Project, an informational forum, and a public hearing, the Air District refused to conduct a CEQA review process.

6.   Petitioners and others presented the Air District with scientific information that the Air District refused to consider regarding the probable environmental and health effects of the Project, including increased emissions of highly toxic chemicals, including dioxins, furans, PAHs, PCBs, hexavalent chromium, and cadmium.

7.   CEQA requires that any project with a potential environmental impact be subject to an environmental assessment process. Further, it requires that projects that will have an impact on the environment— such as the proposal to burn tires and create new toxic emissions— be subjected to a full analysis through an Environmental Impact Report (EIT).

8.   The Air District conducted no CEQ Initial Study and issued neither an EIR nor a Negative Declaration.

9.   The Air District's review of the application to construct the Project does not comply with the requirements of CEQA, because no CEQA review was conducted despite the fact that the decision was discretionary.

10. Respondents' burning of tires may have a significant impact on the environment.

11. The Project will cause irreparable damage to the environment and/or public health. The Project will cause pollution and create new toxic emissions that may damage the environment and may cause health hazards for surrounding residents.

12. If the Air District is not enjoined from authorizing respondent to modify its plant without environmental review, Petitioners will suffer irreparable harm for which there is an adequate remedy at law in that the Respondent will be able to burn tires in its cement kiln releasing new toxic emissions without any CEQA compliance measures or any public review process to analyze the Project's environmental impacts and ways to reduce them, contrary to the requirements of law.

Lawsuits to Overcome Political Inertia: Fighting for Environmental Justice

The Birth of the Environmental Justice Movement

The environmental justice movement is said to have come into being from protests in Warren County, North Carolina in 1982. Warren County, a generally rural area with a largely African American population, had been selected as the site for the burial of 30,000 cubic yards of PCB-contaminated soil. PCBs (polychlorinated biphenyls) had been illegally dumped alongside 14 roadways in North Carolina in 1978. These roadways were cleaned up in 1982 (Geiser and Waneck, 1983). Numerous civil rights groups demonstrated against the dumping, resulting in the arrest of more than 500 protesters (Geiser and Waneck, 1983).

A 1992 study of the *National Law Journal* that examined census data, civil court dockets, and the performance of the Environmental Protection Agency (EPA) found that (1) penalties under hazardous waste laws were significantly higher at sites with the greatest white population, compared to those at sites with the greatest minority population; (2) the disparity under the toxic waste laws was associated with race, not income; (3) 20 percent more time was required for abandoned waste sites in minority communities to be placed on the national priority list under the giant Superfund cleanup program, compared to sites in white areas; (4) the EPA more frequently recommended treatment (the removal of the toxins) in white areas and containment (the walling off of a hazardous waste dump site) in minority areas; and (5) cleanup action at Superfund sites in minority areas often began significantly later than at white sites (Lavelle and Coyle, 1992). The study concluded:

> There is a racial divide in the way the U.S. government cleans up toxic waste sites and punishes polluters. White communities see faster action, better results and stiffer penalties than communities where blacks, Hispanics and other minorities live. This unequal protection often occurs whether the community is wealthy or poor (Lavelle and Coyle, 1992: S1–S2).

The environmental justice movement as it now exists is characterized by four distinguishing features. First, the movement focuses on environmental hazards such as waste facilities and the pollution that results from these facilities (Yamamoto and Lyman, 2001). Second, the movement focuses on the disproportionate distribution of these facilities and efforts to relocate them. Third, the environmental justice movement advocates for the equal representation of communities of color in the administration of environmental laws and policies. Finally, the movement seeks to empower local community members, thereby placing increased pressure on the persons or agencies with decisionmaking authority with respect to a particular issue (Yamamoto and Lyman, 2001). Community action for environmental justice is often spearheaded by women who recognize their neighbors' health problems, are concerned about the health of children, and do not agree that disease is a necessary risk of economic growth (Edelstein, 1988). They often do not see themselves as activists. When attempts at direct community action fail to overcome political inertia, litigation may be seen as the only viable alternative. The case of Woburn, Massachusetts illustrates this multi-faceted approach well.

Woburn, Massachusetts: Leukemia and Litigation

Woburn lies 12 miles to the north of Boston. The per capita income in this town of 37,000 people is only $12,904; less than one-quarter of the adults have graduated from college (Brown and Mikkelsen, 1997). In May of 1979, builders accidentally discovered 184 55-gallon drums in a vacant lot alongside the Aberjona River. Water samples from two contiguous wells, which provided most of the municipal water for East Woburn, were found to be contaminated with extraordinarily high concentrations of trichlorothylene (TCE) and tetrachloroethylene (PCE), both known to cause cancer in laboratory animals. The state ordered that both of the wells be closed. That same year, the U.S. Army Corps of Engineers found dangerous levels of arsenic, lead, and chromium in a protected wetlands area, in violation of the Wetlands Act. By 1980, 12 cases of childhood leukemia had been identified in Woburn, prompting residents to form the citizens' group For a Cleaner

Environment (FACE) in order to mobilize public concern (DiPerna, 1985). FACE worked diligently through the media, the city council, communications with the Centers for Disease Control and Prevention (CDC), and the Massachusetts Department of Public Health to focus public attention on the contamination, the resulting childhood morbidity and mortality, and the responsibilities of the defendant companies (Brown and Mikkelsen, 1997; Harr, 1995). Ultimately, those involved agreed that litigation against the companies responsible for having dumped the toxins must be a necessary component of their efforts:

> It was the only way to go, the only way to make anybody listen. If we left it up to the city or the EPA or any of the governmental agencies, nothing would have ever been accomplished because they are just all—you know, they appoint one commission after another, or a committee to take care of the problem so that it never gets done. So filing the suit was the only thing that I could see that would bring something about really quick and take care of the children (Quoted in Brown and Mikkelsen, 1997: 12).

Lawsuits to Effectuate Change: Fighting Domestic Violence

Lawsuits and Changing Police Attitudes

Advocates for battered women have been notably successful in their use of the courts to effectuate much-needed change. Less than 20 years ago, the following scenario reflected the "typical" police response to the beating of a wife by her husband:

> Police officers are dispatched to a home at 10:30 pm on a Saturday night. The officers are met at the door by an angry woman who is bleeding from the nose. She is extremely agitated and is swearing at the police to get her husband out of the house. The woman explains that her husband hit her because she yelled at him for spending the grocery money. He admits to having hit her, but only after listening to her yell at him "for twenty solid minutes." Both the man and the woman see her behavior as, at least partially, having caused the assault . . . It does not appear that the woman is in immediate danger. The officers talk to both parties until they are calm and ask the man to leave the house for the evening (Pence, 1983: 252).

The well-known case of Jean Balistreri further illustrates what had been the prevailing attitude of law enforcement officers to situations involving battered women (*Balistreri v. Pacifica Police Department*, 1990). Balistreri phoned the police, after having received a severe beating from her husband. Although she had sustained injuries to her nose, mouth, eyes, teeth, and abdomen, the responding officers did not offer her any medical assistance and then convinced her not to file a report. She obtained a restraining order against her former husband in an attempt to halt the continuing harassment and violence. Her ex-husband made harassing phone calls to her and drove his car into her garage, in violation of the court order. He later tossed a firebomb into her home, causing severe damage. The police took 45 minutes to respond to that emergency phone call. Balistreri brought a lawsuit against the police department for their lack of responsiveness (*Balistreri v. Pacifica Police Department*, 1990).

Litigation, however, brought about significant changes. In one case, Tracey Thurman successfully sued the city of Torrington, Connecticut, claiming that her right to equal protection had been violated. Thurman claimed that she had informed the police on several occasions that her husband had threatened to kill her. On the night of a near-fatal attack, her husband stabbed her 13 times while a police officer stood nearby waiting for other officers to arrive on the scene. The court found that the police had failed to provide protection to women who claimed to be abused by their intimate partners and that they did not receive the same level of protection as individuals who had been assaulted by strangers (*Thurman v. City of Torrington*, 1984).

Other lawsuits were brought against police departments for their failure to provide protection to battered women. A number of these lawsuits were premised on the equal protection clause and argued that individuals assaulted by intimate partners were treated differently than those who were assaulted by strangers (*Bartalone v. County of Berrien*, 1986; *Sherrell v. City of Longview*, 1987; *Thurman v. City of Torrington*, 1984; *Watson v. City of Kansas City*, 1988). Other lawsuits claimed that due process rights had been violated where there existed a special, although noncustodial relationship, between the police and the victim, such as where the police had knowledge of an attacker's threats and of the existence of a restraining order and yet failed to protect the victim (*Balistreri v. Pacific Police Department*, 1988). Still other lawsuits claimed that the police had been negligent in instances where there existed a "special relationship" between the police and the victim.

Battered Women's Defense of Self-Defense

Still other inroads have been forged in advocating for battered women by arguments advanced on behalf of women who have been accused of killing their abusive partners. In general, a successful plea of self-defense requires a reasonable belief on the part of the individual committing the killing that he or she was in imminent danger of great bodily harm or death at the time that he or she committed the defensive act. The person accused of the killing, the defendant, must also demonstrate that the only means of escape from this danger was through the use of deadly force. This requirement of objective reasonableness derives from a conceptualization of self-defense as it relates to one-time, face-to-face confrontations between men. However, it does not consider a situation involving the repeated beating and terrorization of a physically weaker individual who has been socialized to refrain from physical violence by a physically stronger individual who has been socialized to value strength and aggressiveness. As a result, a woman who kills her sleeping husband following a violent incident that has been preceded by many other violent incidents may be found to not be in imminent danger; her use of a gun may be found to have been unreasonable, leading to a conviction for murder (*State v. Stewart*, 1988).

Some courts, however, have been made aware of other possible resolutions through arguments presented to them by those advocating on behalf of the accused women. Accordingly, some states permit the reasonableness of a woman's actions to be judged on a subjective basis (*State v. Koss*, 1990; *State v. Leidholm*, 1983; *State v. Warrow*, 1977). Other courts have utilized a two-part test, whereby the individual must have believed that his or her life was in imminent danger (subjective belief) and that belief must have been objectively reasonable from the perspective of an ordinary, reasonable person in a similar situation (*People v. Aris*, 1989; *State v. Gallegos*, 1986; *State v. Kelly*, 1984; *State v. Norman*, 1989). Still other states allow a defense of imperfect self-defense, whereby an individual can be convicted of manslaughter, rather than murder. This defense recognizes that an individual may have believed that she was in imminent danger, while rejecting the reasonableness of that belief (*People v. Humphrey*, 1986; *In re Christian S.*, 1994).

DISCUSSION QUESTIONS

1.   You are concerned with the ability of prisoners in the state prison system to obtain adequate medical care. Discuss the (in)appropriateness of advocacy through the courts as a viable approach to addressing the problem. Support your response.

2.   You are an employee of a nonprofit organization that is concerned with access to health care for underserved populations. Your organization has recently joined with others, on behalf of specified individuals, to support the individuals' lawsuit seeking retribution against various corporations for their role in the use of slave labor prior to Emancipation. Your organization has demonstrated its support through the filing of an *amicus curiae* (friend of the court) brief in the court in which the lawsuit was filed.

a. Is your agency's participation an appropriate use of advocacy through the courts? Why or why not?
b. What, if any, alternative courses of action are available to the plaintiffs? Which, if any, would you recommend and why?

REFERENCES

Austin, R., Schill, M. (1994). Black, brown, red, and poisoned. In R.D. Bullard (Ed.). *Unequal Protection: Environmental Justice and Communities of Color* (pp. 53–74). San Francisco: Sierra Club.

Balistreri v. Pacifica Police Department. (1988). 855 F.2d 1421 (9th Cir.), amended and superseded by 901 F.2d 696 (1990).

Bartalone v. County of Berrien. (1986). 643 F. Supp. 574 (W.D. Mich.).

Brandt, A.M. (1988). AIDS: From social history to social policy. In E. Fee, D.M. Fix (Eds.). *AIDS: The Burdens of History* (pp. 147–189). Berkeley, CA: University of California Press.

Brown, P., Mikkelsen, E.J. (1997). *No Safe Place: Toxic Waste, Leukemia, and Community Action*. Berkeley, CA: University of California Press.

California Public Resources Code. (1996). §§ 21001–21002.1.

Chalk v. United States District Court, C.D. Cal. (1988). 840 F.2d 701 (9th Cir.).

Cook, T.E., Colby, D.C. (1992). The mass-mediated epidemic: The politics of AIDS on the nightly network news. In E. Fee, D.M. Fix (Eds.). *AIDS: The Making of a Chronic Disease* (pp. 84–122). Berkeley, CA: University of California Press.

DiPerna, P. (1985). *Cluster Mystery: Epidemic and the Children of Woburn, Mass*. St. Louis: Mosby.

Dixon v. Superior Court. (1994). 36 Cal. Rptr. 2d 687.

Doe v. Belleville School District No. 118. (1987). 672 F. Supp. 342 (S.D. Ill.).

Doe v. Centinela Hospital. (1988). 57 U.S.L.W. 2034 (C.D. Cal.).

Doe v. Dolton Elementary School District No. 148. (1988). 694 F. Supp. 440 (N.D. Ill.).

Edelstein, M.R. (1988). *Contaminated Communities: The Social and Psychological Impacts of Residential Toxic Exposure*. Boulder, CO: Westview.

Federal Rule of Civil Procedure 23.

Foucault, M. (1979). *Discipline & Punish: The Birth of the Prison*. New York: Vantage Books.

Geiser, K., Waneck, G. (1983). PCBs and Warren County. *Science for the People, 15*, 13–17.

Harr, J. (1995). *A Civil Action*. New York: Vintage Books.

Hurwitz v. New York City Commission on Human Rights. (1988). 142 Misc. 2d 214 (N.Y. Sup. Ct.).

In re Christian S. (1994). 872 P.2d 574.

Lavelle, M., Coyle, M. (1992). Unequal protection. *National Law Journal, Sept. 21*, S1–S2.

Martinez v. School Board of Hillsborough County, Florida. (1989). 861 F.2d 1502 (11th Cir.), reversing 711 F. Supp. 1293 (M.D. Fla. 1988).

Musto, D.F. (1988). Quarantine and the problem of AIDS. In E. Fee, D.M. Fox (Eds.). *AIDS: The Burdens of History* (pp. 67–85). Berkeley, CA: University of California Press.

Oppenheimer, G.M. (1992). Causes, cases, and cohorts: The role of epidemiology in the historical construction of AIDS. In E. Fee, D.M. Fox (Eds.). *AIDS: The Making of a Chronic Disease* (pp. 49–83). Berkeley, CA: University of California Press.

Pence, E. (1983). The Duluth domestic abuse intervention project. *Hamline Law Review, 6*, 247–275.

People v. Aris. (1989). 264 Cal. Rptr. 167 (Cal. App.).

People v. Humphrey. (1986). 921 P.2d 1.

Phipps v. Saddleback Valley Unified School District. (1988). 251 Cal. Rptr. 720 (Cal. App. 4th).

Ray v. School District of DeSoto County. (1987). 666 F. Supp. 1524 (M.D. Fla.).

Raytheon v. Fair Employment and Housing Commission, Estate of Chadbourne. (1989). 261 Cal. Rptr. 197. (Cal. App. 2d).

Robertson v. Granite City Community Unit School District No. 9. (1988). 684 F. Supp. 1002 (S.D. Ill.).

Seitzman v. Hudson River Association. (1987). 513 N.Y.S.2d 148.

Shaw, R. (2001). *The Activist's Handbook: A Primer.* Berkeley, CA: University of California Press.

Sherrell v. City of Longview. (1987). 683 F. Supp. (E.D. Tex.).

Shilts, R. (1987). *And the Band Played On: Politics, People, and the AIDS Epidemic.* New York: St. Martin's Press.

Shuttleworth v. Broward County. (1986). 639 F. Supp. 654, 649 F. Supp. 35 (S.D. Fla.).

State v. Gallegos. (1986). 719 P.2d 1268 (N.M. App.).

State v. Kelly. (1984). 478 A.2d 364 (N.J.).

State v. Koss. (1990). 551 N.E.2d 970 (Ohio).

State v. Leidholm. (1983). 334 N.W.2d 811 (N.D.).

State v. Norman. (1989). 378 S.E.2d 8 (N.C.).

State v. Stewart. (1988). 763 P.2d 572 (Kan.).

State v. Warrow. (1977). 559 P.2d 548 (Wash.).

Thurman v. City of Torrington. (1984). 595 F. Supp. 1521 (D. Conn.).

Watson v. City of Kansas City. (1988). 857 F.2d 690 (10th Cir.).

Yamamoto, E.K., Lyman, J.W. (2001). Racializing environmental justice. *Colorado Law Review, 72,* 311–360.

CHAPTER EIGHT

The Media

"[T]o speak a true word is to transform the world."
(Freire, 1978: 60)

Media, including newspapers, television, radio, newsletters, is powerful; it provides most Americans with much of their information about health and wellness (National Mental Health Association, 2002). The business of the media is both news and entertainment. Newsworthiness of a story, when it does catch the attention of the media, is often transitory, often competing with more sensational stories. The effective use of the media, however, may be critical to the success or failure of community health advocacy efforts. This chapter focuses on the impact of the media, and how to use that impact through media advocacy efforts. Suggestions are provided on how to establish a relationship with the media and various approaches to draw attention to an issue through the media. Numerous examples from the published literature are provided, followed by a case study of media advocacy through the Dangerous Promises campaign.

INFLUENCE OF THE MEDIA

Medical and health news is becoming increasingly visible in the media. Many daily newspapers employ reporters whose specific focus is health or medical or science news, and many television networks have their own medical editor. Television alone may be considered by some to be the single most important and valued source of health information (Gibson, Hudson and Watts, 1999).

Historically, the media has had a significant influence on community health and health promotion. A study of protection motivation theory in the context of mass media reports about a hazard found that mass media can influence through the use of dramatic portrayals and news articles and broadcasts an individual's intent to change behavior and to seek additional information (Neuwirth, Dunwoody, and Griffin, 2000). The greater the illustrated severity of the hazard, the greater the individual's desire to acquire more information. The combination of information about severity, levels of risk and effective responses results in greater change in intentions and actions to modify behavior.

Media coverage has played a key role in the mental health consumer movement. On May 13, 1946, *Life Magazine* published a 13-page article entitled, "Bedlam 1946, Most US Hospitals Are Ashamed and Disgraced," which included photographs and details of a protest by individuals working in mental hospitals against the horrendous conditions there. Shocking details of treatment in a psychiatric hospital served as the basis of a best-selling novel, *The Snake Pit*, published in the same year, and later a movie by the same name. Undoubtedly influenced by the attention brought by the media coverage and advocacy, Congress passed the National Mental Health Act, establishing the National Institute of Mental Health (Foulks, 2000).

Negative publicity through mass media coverage of the pill and the intrauterine devide (IUD) seems to correlate directly with discontinuation rates for these two contraceptive methods between 1970 and 1975. News stories highlighting negative consequences resulted in an almost immediate but short-lived decrease in utilization, while the cumulative effect of more general coverage through documentaries, features, stories, and editorials supported a longer-term and sustained trend of discontinuation (Jones, Beniger and Westoff, 1980).

Public opinion about health and treatment is often molded by the news media. If the information presented is incorrect, incomplete or otherwise biased, public perceptions can quickly become distorted. Berlin and Malin (1991) report one such instance regarding the public's perception about the success or failure of psychiatric rehabilitation. Media coverage in this instance focused on some treatment failures with alleged criminal recidivism without presenting all of the extenuating information or examining treatment successes. This issue was complicated by the unwillingness of clinic staff to be interviewed or correct misinformation, which involved the release of confidential patient information and would have violated patient-psychiatrist privilege. The authors concluded that a biased presentation that focused only on the treatment failures could potentially have a negative impact on the overall promotion of community health with serious consequences for patients, health care workers, and society at large.

Spontaneous news stories with health implications can unexpectedly enhance community health promotion and advocacy efforts, although the impact is usually short-lived. A study by Fink and colleagues (1978) examined the impact of nationwide media coverage of the breast surgery of the wives of the President and Vice President of the United States on responses to a breast cancer screening program. Enrollment and participation in the program increased significantly in late 1974 at the time of the mass media coverage; rates declined to previous levels after the media coverage ended. These responses were fairly uniform among all demographic groups, with news coverage apparently reaching and impacting all segments of the female population. This is in contrast to most studies that show that increased media coverage of a health issue is more likely to have an impact only on those already concerned and affected by the issue. The high profile of the Presidential and Vice-Presidential wives may have been instrumental in opening the discussion of this "taboo" health problem. This study also underscores the importance of informing the public about both an issue and how to obtain related services.

PROACTIVELY USING THE MEDIA: MEDIA ADVOCACY

Elements of Media Advocacy

Effective community health advocacy needs to be able to use the media and proactively harness its power and influence; it can accomplish this through media advocacy. Woodruff (1996: 335) defines media advocacy "as the strategic use of mass media in support of community organizing to advance public policy by applying pressure to policymakers. It focuses media attention on those who have the power to change policy. Rooted in community advocacy, media advocacy attempts to harness the power of the media for social change."

As a new paradigm in approaching public health, Russell and colleagues (1995) suggest that health educators use media advocacy to encourage political action and change. In moving the focus of public health from individual blame to the underlying societal and institutional context, media advocacy is a source of power that enables communities to define and publicize their concerns and to build support for changes in public policy (DeJong, 1996). Additionally, media advocacy increases the efficacy of advocates in addressing the relevant environmental factors (Woodruff, 1996).

Woodruff (1996) summarizes five precepts, based on the work of Walleck, Dorfman, Jernigan and Themba, as critical to the practice of media advocacy: (1) the campaign must be based on issues and concerns affecting the health and well-being of the community, as identified by the community; (2) media advocacy must emphasize the broader context in which health problems arise, rather than focusing solely on the individuals with the problem; (3) the campaign must focus and maintain the attention of the media, while ensuring that the message is appropriately framed; (4) media advocates must understand that news programs draw their audiences by entertaining them. To generate initial interest from the media, the story often needs to focus on individual victimization or conflict (DeJong, 1996; Woodruff, 1996); and (5) the ability to frame or focus the media coverage of issues is critical (Mosher, 1999).

Once the media is engaged, media advocates must reframe the issues from the individual perspective to the larger public health policy issue, using appropriate images, words, and symbols. These may take the form of media "bites," which are brief, quotable statements; visual images; and "social math," which explains statistical information in a relevant context (Woodruff, 1996). Media advocacy may actually reflect a conflict between competing frames (DeJong, 1996).

Matching Method, Message, and Audience

Different audiences may respond to different types of media. In their work with the Community Trials Project to reduce alcohol-related trauma, Treno and Holder (1997b) found significant differences in the populations attracted to television and to newspapers and in the extent to which they were exposed to the issue in either media. The authors concluded that television appears to reach those who are less affluent and less well-educated; these individuals are least likely to be exposed to print news media. However, opinion leaders in positions to influence policy change are more likely to be receptive to print media. Media advocacy efforts may benefit from selectively using different media to target specific audiences.

In addition, a telephone survey conducted by Gibson and colleagues (1999) found that, although viewers placed a higher value on televised health care information than they did on other mass media, recall was found to be generally poor, with most respondents unable to name the topic of the televised report they had viewed, the program name or the program sponsor. Recall may have improved if the televised information is related more directly to individual viewers' specific needs and interests, but the study did not address this option.

A long-term media advocacy campaign must also consider the differences in the impact and utilization of special news and general media coverage. Special news events are used to gain access to the media in order to highlight an issue or to begin public debate. Conversely, general media coverage provides a more general treatment of problems and trends and often relies on documentaries, features, stories or editorials. General media coverage is more likely to have a gradual and lasting effect on behavioral change (Jones, Beniger and Westoff, 1980).

Advocacy efforts tend to follow an adversarial model, highlighting the struggles of the "little guy" or community members working for social justice versus big government and big business. Media advocacy can be strategic in creating both confrontation to highlight an issue and in suggesting reconciliation to effectuate policy change. Generating and sustaining media attention that makes opponents uncomfortable helps to ensure that the focus remains on the community interests as both sides work to resolve the issue. While this approach is empowering to many, it may not be comfortable for everyone or in some settings, and can create divisiveness within the group. Group members must agree on an acceptable level of confrontation during their advance planning for the media advocacy campaign, with periodic reassessment throughout the campaign (Woodruff, 1996).

The media can be used strategically to mobilize support for community projects along with policy change. As described by Treno and Holder (1997a) in the Community Trials Project to reduce alcohol-related trauma, the media was used to increase public awareness of the issue in general and to communicate that community response to key policy makers who effected needed change. Publicity generated by project activities, including images of DUI checkpoints on television and in print, played a much more extensive role in mobilizing community response than was originally anticipated. News coverage through special local community events emphasized local community ownership.

Media advocacy for public health can also take the form of social marketing to counteract the media and marketing strategies of for-profit business which may promote or encourage unhealthy behaviors to sell their products. Mosher (1999), in addressing alcohol policy and young adults, examined media strategies used by the alcohol industry to target young adults. Creative media messages developed by the industry convey a seemingly contradictory message, that *everyone* should drink alcoholic beverages to express their individuality. The industry also seeks to identify cultural icons, holidays, symbols of freedom, and athletic excellence with consumption of their product. A public health response can employ media strategies focusing on the same concepts, but with positive images and messages that challenge youth and young adults to improve their surrounding environment. One way to debunk the industry's marketing campaign is to expose its focus on profit and its contribution to health problems.

Media advocacy has traditionally used the media to reach policymakers (Woodruff, 1996). To effectively accomplish this, media advocates must acknowledge that news making is a business with certain constraints. Television news, in particular, is expected to be profitable, but its very nature does not allow adequate time and resources to research stories. Appropriately nurtured, however, these deficits can be turned into an opportunity to assist reporters by providing them with the necessary research or by creating the stories for them. Media advocates should provide journalists with the information that they need, which includes visual displays, succinct quotes, and an interesting and newsworthy "spin." The more complete the menu of items that can be given to a reporter, the more likely the story will be reflective of what the advocates need. It is important that relationships be built with reporters and journalists to ensure that supportive stories that focus on the broader context will be included. While some believe that media advocacy efforts should also focus on reforming news media to become more responsible and less sensationalistic, an aggressive critique could seriously jeopardize the existing partnership (Woodruff, 1996).

Advocates and organizers working for policy change should proceed cautiously in deciding what type of media advocacy strategy to use or even whether to use the media at all. While media advocacy can be used to mobilize and advance a community health agenda, it is important to remember that this also may cast a spotlight on the organization, its staff and activities; all members need to understand and have buy-in on the strategy used. In his review of a media advocacy strategy employed by MADD (Mothers Against Drunk Driving) Massachusetts to influence the State legislative agenda, Dejong (1996) reported that the media exposed an apparent "schism" in attitude toward these efforts between local grassroots members and staff at the state level. The state leadership of MADD failed to recognize the differing level of tolerance of its grassroots members for the approach advocated at the state level.

TECHNIQUES AND STRATEGIES FOR
MEDIA ADVOCACY

Advance Preparations

Following are suggestions for preparing for, contacting, and utilizing the media.

The Arizona Partnership for Immunization (TAPI, 2001) suggests that, before contacting the media, basic tools be prepared and assembled that will facilitate a rapid and efficient response to a media call. This preparation will also allow the group to take advantage of unexpected spontaneous media stories related to the topic. This preparation includes a Fact Sheet, Source List, Talking Points, Question and Answer Sheet, and Press Briefing Packet (Press Kit).

The Fact Sheet is a one or two page document that briefly and visually conveys the main messages. It permits an expedient response to a media request for information and can be used for general distribution to the press and public.

A Source List is a roster of individuals available to speak on the issue and who can be trusted to stay "on message" for quotes to reporters looking for other contacts on the issue.

"Talking Points" refers to the main messages written out on paper. They should be available for staff and supporters to use in every contact with the press. Ideally, they should include no more than four main messages, be only one or two pages in length, and be clear and easy to read.

The Question and Answer Sheet ("Q and A") offers winning answers to most-often-asked, difficult and controversial questions on the issue. It can also be used for general distribution to the press and public.

A Press List is a listing of all media outlets in the area, including newspapers, radio stations, and television stations. The database should be set up so that information can be retrieved quickly for each item and should include the media market, address, and the reporter's name, focus (for example, health, business), phone number, fax number, and e-mail address. For publicity around events planned well in advance, the National Association of Social Workers (NASW, 2002) suggests a second list of calendar editors and public service directors whose deadlines range from 3 to 6 weeks before an event; contacts on the first list can be used to generate coverage during and after an event.

There are many ways to build and tailor the press list. Bacon's Information, Inc. publishes catalogs with contact information for print and broadcast media, including news editors and reporters throughout North America. Calling the general number of a paper, television station or radio station is also a good place to begin. Most, if not all, media maintain their own web sites on the Internet. Web-based searches can elicit contact details for these sites. E-mail is becoming more popular with journalists and should be utilized as a component of the media strategy. ACT UP (2002) emphasizes highlighting local newspaper reporters who might cover the issue or political demonstrations; these names can be acquired by contacting the papers' news editors. Note should be made of television and radio stations and reporters who have covered related stories. Reporters from the wire services should also be included; this information may be obtained from a regional listing for Associated Press, United Press International Reuters, and any other wire services.

A Press Briefing Packet or Press Kit is a pocket folder containing all of the documents to be given to a reporter to assist in his or her coverage of the issue. The name of the organization, logo and contact information should be on the outside of the folder. Contents could include a letter of introduction, business card(s), Fact Sheet, a detailed explanation and background material on the issue, Source List, a calendar of upcoming events, articles or editorials highlighting or in support of the issue, background on the organization and program history, brochures and flyers, the organization or program newsletter, charts or graphics, local statistics, any awards or recognition the program or organization has received, and color slides and/or black and white photographs, if available. If feasible, press kits should be sent to media contacts two weeks before a planned media or other event and also available at the event (TAPI, 2001; ACT UP, 2002).

The Spokesperson, the Message, and the Story

Publicity should be assigned specifically to one or several individuals, with local spokespersons readily available for radio, television and newspaper interviews. For a spokesperson on a specific issue, it is generally a good idea to use people affected by a policy, for example, doctors and patients on treatment-related issues and police officials or affected citizens on community safety issues. It is particularly effective to rely on individuals who have a high public profile already, if feasible.

ACT UP (2002) suggests that the message be simple and singular, e.g., "needle exchange programs save lives." The message should focus on a topic more likely to attract media attention; that attention can then be used to address underlying or background issues of importance. Values such as security of the family and justice should be addressed. Facts must be correct and well-documented to withstand intense scrutiny, and solutions to the issue should be highlighted. Stories of injustice framed by a human face may be effective, especially for generally unsympathetic reporters. To receive media attention, advocates should express anger and outrage, and be oppositional. In response to the media's mission to provide news as well as to entertain, stories should be pitched as entertainment, with a cast of characters and a story.

ACT UP (2002) recommends that a story be developed by imaging the story first and then working backwards. Debate over the issue raised should be anticipated; responses to opposing arguments and ways to influence and steer the debate need to be considered in advance. It is extremely important to react and respond to questions or challenges; if one reporter calls, it may be indicative of interest by others as well, and can be an opportunity for a press release or other strategy to highlight the issue through the media. Media advocates should be alert to capitalize on anything blatantly incorrect or misleading that is advanced by opponents. ACT UP (2002) encourages finding ways to take the story to the national level, which may occur after a period of regional coverage. Another important strategy to magnify public awareness and debate over the issues is to have the theme portrayed on popular television series.

Contacting the Media

Using the press list, each reporter should be contacted by phone or e-mail, and an appointment scheduled. E-mail can be used to create a sense of urgency and immediacy. If unable to visit him/her in person, a phone conversation can also be effective in creating an impression. The press kit and other general information should be given or mailed to the reporter, with a follow-up phone call made to ensure receipt (University of North Texas, 2002).

Press Releases

A press release is a written pitch for an issue. It should be no longer than one page, beginning with the name and phone number of the media contact person. The first paragraph describes who, what, where, when, and why, followed by additional information on the what and the why in the second paragraph, and then more details on the issue. ACT UP (2002) recommends the use of strong adjectives and a dramatic, emotional quote.

The press release should be e-mailed or faxed to media outlets; public service announcements (PSAs) should be sent to calendar editors and public service directors. ACT UP (2002) suggests that the press release be sent so that it is received 24 to 36 hours in advance of an event. Priority should be given to media contacts used in the past or recently discovered. In lieu of having specific contacts with some media, it should be sent to news editors, metro editors and assignment editors for newspapers, television and radio, and also the regional wire service office. The press release can also be sent, as appropriate, to church bulletins; to company newsletters of major area employers; to community events calendars; to special interest publications, including ethnic, feminist or gay/ptlesbian publications; to high school and college papers, and other smaller newspapers; and to radio stations or other media outlets that may target an audience that would be particularly interested in the issue. Local cable television stations should be contacted to ask about listing events and activities on their community bulletin board (NASW, 2002; ACT UP, 2002).

A press release that is unaccompanied by some additional form of promotion is typically ignored or thrown away; follow-up is, therefore, extremely important. A call should be made a few hours after the press release is faxed or e-mailed or soon after it would be expected to arrive in the mail; if the fax or e-mail is sent in the afternoon, the call can be made the next morning. The call can be used to ensure receipt of the press release or PSA. If it has been misplaced or it has not been received, an offer should be made to send it again. This must then be done immediately. Alternatively, the call may be used to inquire if the story will be covered. If so, the assignment editor may be able to provide information on which reporter has the assignment. If not, this may be used as an opportunity to encourage coverage. A press release sent to a specific reporter creates a reason to call and talk to him/her about it. ACT UP (2002) recommends that the advocate be friendly and persistent, and avoid using criticism or guilt as a mechanism for obtaining story coverage.

Letters to the Editor and Op-Ed Columns

Letters to the editor are specifically useful for community newspapers, and should reiterate the Talking Points developed for the campaign or program. Sample letters-to-the-editor may be developed for members and supporters to model their own letters (NASW, 2002). In terms of the op-ed column, ACT UP (2002) recommends that timing take greater priority than quality, that the column should include a local perspective, be as personal as possible, and be limited to no more than three sentences.

The Arab American Institute (2002: www.aaiusa.org/newsandviews/ contactingthe media/ :1–2) offers the following suggestions to increase the likelihood that letters to the editor and op-ed pieces will be published:

(1)   Be timely. Respond while the issue is still fresh in the minds of journalists and their audiences. Send your letter no later than a week after the article appears in print or is broadcast.

(2)   Be direct. The opening paragraph should contain your main point. You want the reader to be able to quickly identify your message.

(3)   Be concise. Your letter's length will affect its chances of being

published. Most publications will not print more than three short paragraphs.

(4) Use words that convey a firm and resolute stance. If you're writing a letter critical of news coverage, use adjectives such as distorted, inaccurate, out-of-context, one-sided, skewed. If you are complimenting an article or editorial, make sure you note its fairness, balance and/or thoroughness.

(5) Stay cool. Hostile or overly emotional language in your letter will hurt your chances rather than help them. Stating your case in a convincing fashion is the most important criterion for getting published.

(6) Spread the word. Don't just send your letter to the editor. You can maximize its impact if you send a copy to other people responsible for the article, such as the reporter, foreign editor or syndicated columnist, as well as those mentioned in the article, such as a congress member or public official.

(7) Claim credit. Before publishing a letter, most papers will call to verify that you wrote it. Make sure you include your full name, title, address and daytime phone number in the letter.

(8) Follow up. Inquire about the status of your letter with a phone call or letter. If you submit a letter in the future, the editor may remember you and give you more immediate consideration.

Interviews with Reporters

ACT UP (2002) recommends that those participating in interviews with reporters be friendly, have a sense of humor, be straightforward, and provide a story "hook." Good work by the reporter should be acknowledged; reporters rarely receive compliments and often receive complaints about their work. This will create a more receptive environment for him/her to listen to you. Don't make demands. Give him/her the press kit and familiarize him/her with the issue and why it's important; don't assume that they already know about the issue, even if it is their area of interest. Give the reporter a good interview, the right type of information or other contacts that will make it easier for the reporter to write the story (Arno and Feiden, 1992), and accurate information. Stay with the message, use the Talking Points, and mold the agenda for the interview with your answers to questions posed. A response is not required for every question, particularly if the intention is to take the discussion in a different direction or to a different angle. Shorter sentences or responses may be better; try not to get bogged down in the details. For television interviews, you should dress in neutral colors, such as gray, blue, or brown, avoiding patterns and/or large or ostentatious jewelry; request that the interview be in natural light if possible; talk in sound bites; avoid using "uh" or "er" to fill in pauses between comments; and request a copy on video or audio for later evaluation.

If the reporter receives a good, productive interview, he/she will be more likely to call again in the future, and a contact is established. Consider any single contact with a reporter in the context of developing a mutually beneficial relationship for the future. If the reporter does a good job covering or writing about the issue, let him/her know; also let him/her know if anything in the story is incorrect. You should make yourself easily available to contact for an interview or information. Working against demanding deadlines, reporters may move on to someone or something else to fill the gap if they can't reach you, and an opportunity will be lost.

You should cultivate individual reporters, develop personal relationships, return calls promptly, and assist in finding other contacts or tips for reporters' stories, even if it's on an unrelated issue. Send any articles, statistics or reports you receive that you think would be newsworthy or provide more clarification on an issue to the reporter. A reporter who is familiar with you and favorable to the issue will be more willing to listen in the future. Knowing a reporter will also assist in knowing how to pitch a story to gain their interest and help him/her sell it to his/her editor. In the case of reporters who are difficult or hostile, try to find a way around them; complaints to supervisors are generally unproductive. It may sometimes be better to pitch a new story, rather than try to have an old news story corrected. You can give those who have done erroneous or biased reporting in the past a chance to redeem themselves by educating them on the issues.

If possible, call a print reporter before 3 p.m.; after that time, they will most likely be focused on meeting a deadline. Ask if he/she is able to talk; if not, try to schedule another time to call. If he/she indicates no interest in the issue, ask why and who else might be contacted. The provision of stories and contacts helps a reporter to do a good job; this may ultimately be appreciated.

Staging Media Events

Media coverage of staged events like demonstrations can be used effectively to highlight and keep an issue in the public eye. ACT UP is considered a master of the media event or demonstration, in combination with acts of non-violent civil disobedience. ACT UP even received an award for street theater from New York City's Dance Theater Workshop (Arno and Feiden, 1992). ACT UP (2002) offers several tips on planning for such events.

(1)   Schedule the event/demonstration to coincide with a holiday or a time that media and public interest in the story would be higher. Tie it to current events in the news.

(2)   Cultivate the participation of the media. Send a press release to media contacts several weeks before the event and request that they announce the event or write an article about it. Send formal invitations to reporters and editors who have received the press releases; send a few photos of any VIPs who will be attending. Call to find out if any additional information is needed. Encourage advance, day-of, and follow-up coverage of the issue and event, and thank media personnel after the event for any media coverage received.

(3)   Choose a "media friendly" time of day and day of the week. Noon or earlier, Monday through Thursday, is ideal. Newspapers and the wire services close their stories by 5 or 6 p.m., and the event needs to end by 2 or 3 p.m. in order for the story to appear in the next day's papers. Local television news may be able to tape up until an hour or two before air time or even broadcast live, but this is also riskier. Keep in mind that the earlier in the day the story is "in the can," the more time there is to work on the story with the producer or on-camera reporter, creating a better opportunity to ensure that the message is clearly spelled out. Staging an event Monday through Thursday is more likely to result in the story breaking the next day while the targeted policymaker is in his or her official location, although Saturday is likely to provide wider Sunday paper coverage.

(4)   Plan clear, dramatic visuals for the event/demonstration. Like a sound bite, a concise, interesting visual, such as a photograph or video, increases the chances of media coverage or air play that catches public interest and attention.

(5)   Designate several individuals as liaisons to specifically work with the media at the event/demonstration. These media liaisons need to identify the reporters, introduce themselves, find out who they are and where they're from, ask to see their press identification, offer them press kits, and ask if they need anything and/or would like to interview someone. Reporters are usually identified by press credentials hanging around their necks or by the notebooks, cameras and/or tape recorders that they may be carrying. The liaison should get the reporter's name and contact information

in order to offer follow-up assistance with his/her story after the event, and to add him/her to the media contact list if he/she is not already on it. If interviews are requested, the liaison directs the reporter to individuals who are known to be willing and able to articulate the issues clearly and concisely. If civil disobedience is part of the event/demonstration, it is important to have the press witness it. In the case of police misconduct, reporters should be directed to it. "Reporters" who have no press identification or refuse to show it should be considered suspicious, especially if they are filming or taking photographs; they may be law enforcement or members of groups opposed to the issue. Often, they will stop filming or photographing if pressed for their identification.

(6)   Following the event/demonstration, ensure that the organization's media contact phone is staffed for several hours to respond to reporters who may have questions as they write their story. This may also be an opportunity to inform the reporter of any follow-up activity as a consequence of the event/demonstration of which they may not be aware, such as civil disobedience, arrests, or counter-protests. A wrap-up press release describing what happened may also be considered.

Public Service and Paid Advertising: Social Marketing

The use of advertising in the media may be an effective tool to consider in a campaign to promote and advocate for community health. Keiser (1991), in a review of the PSA medias' marketing techniques for "America Responds to AIDS" (ARTA) employed by the Centers for Disease Control and Prevention (CDC), suggests the following model for campaigns in health communications. First, a clear dominant message that is closely linked to the overall theme or direction of the campaign and its target audience must be identified. Support materials and high-profile spokespersons can be used to reinforce the message. Next, the campaign should be launched through a combination of several methods, including advance media briefings, news conferences, and video news releases. Partners, such as states, national organizations, and community-based organizations, are used to sustain the marketing of the campaign in the development and implementation stages. Briefings with public service directors, before and after the commencement of the campaign, and the provision of campaign materials in the form of "broadcast quality tapes and camera-ready artwork" ensure the continued exposure of campaign messages.

Using this model, ARTA's media marketing campaign created and fostered a national media agenda on AIDS and established the government as a credible source of public health information. Attention fostered through the news media deliberately and consistently resulted in increased use of the PSA materials, and the public received important basic information on the prevention of HIV (Keiser, 1991).

It has been suggested by commercial advertising research that only two to three exposures to a message are needed to produce message recall and, in some cases, effectuate a behavioral response. However, similar research has not been conducted in the context of public health messages. Jason and colleagues (1993) concluded that mass media could effectively reach urban intravenous drug users (IVDUs) with AIDS prevention messages. A group of Baltimore "street" IVDUs, participants in a Baltimore IVDU cohort study, demonstrated a significant degree of contact with all forms of mass media. Fifty-three percent of 353 IVDUs reported that they watched news programs, and 47% indicated that they learned the most about AIDS from television, suggesting that targeted media messages aired at appropriate times could be a cost-effective strategy to supplement the HIV prevention efforts of public health departments. The researchers recommended that media-based approaches be incorporated into HIV prevention activities and that staff be trained to interact and collaborate with the media. The willingness of media policy makers to air messages on IDVU-specific topics, such as sexual abstinence, condom use, or safer drug use practices, varied considerably by media type and range, with greater support on the local level compared to the national, and for radio compared to television.

MEDIA ADVOCACY IN ACTION: CASE STUDY

Woodruff (1996) describes a successful media advocacy effort to highlight the impact of alcohol advertising that utilized messages promoting violence against women and to prevent the continued use of these messages. The Dangerous Promises campaign was premised on the belief that sexist advertising images contribute to an environment that condones violence against women. Media advocacy was used to press the alcohol industry to eliminate the use of sexist images of women in their advertising and promotions.

The Dangerous Promises campaign recognizes that men's violence toward women is rooted in cultural socialization. Violence against women can range from battering and sexual assault to more subtle emotional control and verbal harassment. It is the second leading cause of injury for women and the leading cause for those 15 to 44 years of age. It is considered an insidious epidemic in that it is often inflicted by loved ones. Counselors have reported that men who batter women believe that violence can legitimately be used to solve problems, and that men should be strong and in control, especially with women.

While acknowledging that no strong empirical link exists between sexist advertising and violence, sexist advertising is clearly seen to reinforce and perpetuate images of women as submissive and dependent, as objects that men can control. Advertising often shapes expectations about sexual and gender-based behavior, creating "dangerous promises." While not directly causing the abuse, acceptance of these images by men may be an important element in violence against women. The actual consumption of the alcohol itself seems to be permissive of a wide range of sexist behaviors and has been documented as a co-factor in battering and abuse.

The Dangerous Promises campaign focuses on alcohol advertising, holding alcohol makers accountable for the messages they promote about their products. The campaign targeted the codes of advertising ethics of the three major alcohol trade associations: the Beer Institute, the Wine Institute, and the Distilled Spirits Council of the United States (DISCUS). While association membership and compliance with the code of ethics is voluntary, the associations still wield considerable clout. Before the start of the campaign, none of these codes addressed the depiction of women or violence.

Volunteer advocates began the Dangerous Promises campaign in 1990 with the Trauma Foundation in San Francisco and the Los Angeles Commission on Assaults Against Women and soon expanded to San Diego, where efforts were led by the Center for Women's Studies and Services and the Institute for Health Advocacy. The three branches have similar goals and methods, but each has developed its own timeline and approach. Initial efforts in all three cities focused on community organizing and coalition building with organizational allies to increase community awareness and to show local media that there was broad support for the initiative.

The campaign sought the amendment of the code of ethics of the three alcohol trade associations to include guidelines relating to the themes of sex and violence and the manner in which women are portrayed. Specific language for these changes was created and adopted by the coalition. In November, 1992 the coalition wrote to each of the trade associations, asking each to include these guidelines in their respective code of ethics. While receiving evasive responses from the Beer Institute and DISCUS, the Wine Institute met with coalition representatives and established a task force to examine the issue, and ultimately adopted the main points of the coalition's proposed code in September 1993.

The coalition next focused on media advocacy strategies to pressure the other alcohol institutes. Advocates developed paid counter-advertising to create controversy and thereby substantial media coverage and air time that they could not afford to purchase on their own. Billboards were developed with images of women and these messages: "Hey Bud—Stop Using Our Cans to Sell Yours" (Los Angeles) and "Bloodweiser, King of Tears— Selling Violence Against Women" (San Francisco). Billboard companies in the San Francisco Bay area and Los Angeles refused to carry the ads. The story became newsworthy because of the inherent irony presented by the situation: a coalition of nonprofit agencies was denied the right to buy space for two small anti-violence advertisements, but alcohol companies spent more than $2 billion a year to promote their products. The San Diego chapter, financed by the Alliance Healthcare Foundation, successfully used the same ad planned for Los Angeles, but without the "Hey Bud." Twenty billboards in the region displayed the ad from January to March 1994.

In the fall of 1993, the campaign moved forward on the three fronts to pitch the issue to the local media, resulting in extensive coverage on all fronts and elevating the issue significantly on the media agenda. In October 1993, a news conference was held by the campaign in Los Angeles to publicly thank the Wine Institute for adopting its new code language and to criticize the Beer Institute and DISCUS for their lack of responsiveness. Journalists in the San Francisco Bay Area were invited to see the controversial anti-violence campaign that local billboard companies refused to run. San Diego advocates conducted a 6-month media campaign that included talk radio appearances, in-depth interviews with selected journalists, and a news conference to launch the billboard campaign. All San Diego steering committee and advisory board members were trained in all aspects of media advocacy, with media events occurring over many months to keep the local media focused on the issue.

The coalition advocates used each media contact to frame the issue with a few key points: "Sexism is a root cause of violence against women"; "Sexist alcohol ads reinforce myths that contribute to violence against women"; and "Alcohol companies should stop using such dangerous messages to promote their products." These messages were conveyed through sound bites such as "Alcohol ads imply that if you buy the beer, you get the girl." Coalition members offered reporters numerous examples of offensive alcohol ads as well as copies of the counter-ads, ensuring good visuals for extensive television coverage. "Social math" was effectively used to compare domestic violence to drug violence statistics.

Overall, media response was significant and positive. Advocates were able to access journalists relatively easily, and media turnout was high for the various events. The story was covered by seven television news broadcasts in San Francisco and San Diego; 20 articles appeared in a variety of print media. Most coverage portrayed the public health perspective of the story with the key messages and policy goals stressed by the campaign spokespersons, while the alcohol industry's perspective was virtually absent. The television coverage, in particular, utilized the campaign's sound bites and social math.

The treatment of the issue as a serious topic by the media and the early support of the Wine Industry helped to create public legitimacy for the campaign. Media attention allowed continuing dialogue with the industry. Early in 1994, the coalition successfully reopened discussions on their respective codes of ethics with the Beer Institute and DISCUS. The Beer Institute agreed to reexamine their code, and DISCUS adopted a modified version of the points recommended by the coalition. In tandem with these successes, San Diego also experienced positive changes in local advertising practices.

The Dangerous Promises campaign experienced great success in accessing the media and positively framing news stories in ways that supported and advanced their agenda. Media advocacy, though, is only one tool; it is rarely successful if it becomes a campaign's sole focus. The campaign's advocates acknowledged that continued success would not be able to stand on media advocacy strategies alone because significantly more energy is needed to keep an issue on the media agenda than to get it there. Ongoing community organizing and coalition building are critical elements in any long-term process of change, together with continual assessment and evaluation of policy goals and objectives.

DISCUSSION QUESTIONS

1. Describe the key elements of a successful media advocacy campaign.
2. Map out a model media advocacy campaign on the efficacy and need for a legally sanctioned syringe exchange program in your community. Describe the proposed components and steps to plan and implement the campaign.

REFERENCES

ACT UP (AIDS Coalition to Unleash Power) (2002). New York, NY (January 31, 2002); http://www.actupny.org.
Arab American Institute (2002). Washington, D.C. (January 25, 2002); http://www.aaiusa.org

Arno, P.S., Feiden, K.L. (1992). *Against the Odds: The Story of AIDS, Drug Development, Politics and Profits.* New York: HarperCollins.

Berlin, F.S., Malin, H.M. (1991). Media distortion of the public's perception of recidivism and psychiatric rehabilitation. *American Journal of Psychiatry, 148,* 1572–1576.

DeJong, W. (1996). MADD Massachusetts versus Senator Burke: A media advocacy case study. *Health Education Quarterly, 23,* 318–329.

Fink, R., Roeser, R., Venet, W., Strax, P., Venet, L., Lacher, M. (1978). Effects of news events on response to a breast cancer screening program. *Public Health Reports, 93,* 318–327.

Foulks, E.F. (2000). Advocating for persons who are mentally ill: A history of mutual empowerment of patients and profession. *Administration and Policy in Mental Health, 27,* 353–367.

Gibson, R., Hudson, J.C., Watts, L. (1999). Low recall of local television health care news segment topics, sponsors and program names. *Health Marketing Quarterly, 17,* 55–65.

Jason, J., Solomon, L., Celentano, D.D., Vlahov, D. (1993). Potential use of mass media to reach urban intravenous drug users with AIDS prevention messages. *The International Journal of the Addictions, 28,* 837–851.

Jones, E.F., Beniger, J.R., Westoff, C.F. (1980). Pill and IUD discontinuation in the United States, 1970–1975: The influence of the media. *Family Planning Perspectives, 12,* 293–300.

Keiser, N.H. (1991). Strategies of media marketing for "America Responds to AIDS" and applying lessons learned. *Public Health Reports, 106,* 623–627.

Mosher J.F. (1999). Alcohol policy and the young adult: Establishing priorities, building partnerships, overcoming barriers. *Addiction, 94,* 357–369.

NASW (National Association of Social Workers) (2002). Washington, D.C. (January 10, 2002); http://www.naswdc.org.

National Mental Health Association (2002). Alexandria, VA (February 14, 2002); http://www. nmha.org.

Neuwirth, K., Dunwoody, S., Griffin, R.J. (2000). Protection motivation and risk communication. *Risk Analysis, 20,* 721–734.

Russell, A., Voas, R.B., Dejong, W., Chaloupka, M. (1995). MADD rates the states: A media advocacy event to advance the agenda against alcohol-impaired driving. *Public Health Reports, 110,* 240–245.

TAPI (The Arizona Partnership for Immunization) (2001). Phoenix, AZ (May 22, 2001); http://www.hs.state.az.us/tapii/tapii6.htm

Treno, A.J., Holder, H.D. (1997a). Community mobilization: Evaluation of an environmental approach to local action. *Addiction, 92,* S173–S187.

Treno, A.J., Holder, H.D. (1997b). Community mobilization, organizing, and media advocacy: A discussion of methodological issues. *Evaluation Review, 21,* 166–190.

University of North Texas Center for Parent Education (2002). Denton, TX (January 14, 2002); http://www.unt.edu/cpe.

Woodruff, K. (1996). Alcohol advertising and violence against women: A media advocacy case study. *Health Education Quarterly, 23,* 330–345.

CHAPTER NINE

Evaluating the Advocacy Effort

"'So so' is good, very good, very excellent good; and yet it is not, it is but so."
William Shakespeare, *As You Like It*, V, i, 26.

The few studies that look at evaluation of advocacy efforts can be found in the literature examining community-based organizing and mobilization and media advocacy (also known as social communications by some authors). It is increasingly important for nonprofit organizations to develop some capacity to engage in strategic communications activities to both further the mission of the organization as well as to educate the public about specific problems and ways in which the broader community can be involved in the solution to the problem (Weiss, 2001). Accordingly, this chapter includes evaluation of communication campaigns which were part of larger advocacy efforts.

Weiss (2001) defines strategic communications as including a broad range of activities, such as grassroots organizing, coalition building, and communications campaigns which use the mass media to advance a social or public policy initiative. Strategic communications campaigns can inform and build public support for programs, thereby creating not only public demand for the types of services needed but increased public investment for the services. Media advocacy is not considered to be a stand-alone strategy and, to be effective, must be part of a larger community mobilization framework (Woodruff, 1996). Woodruff notes that if the advocacy does not rest on the true concerns of the community, it will fail to compel community members and journalists will find the goals and the spokespeople less credible.

Oftentimes, evaluation of advocacy efforts relies on whether the final goal was reached, for example, whether the effort was successful in obtaining a positive vote, whether more people volunteered for an activity, et cetera. However, by focusing on the ultimate goal, important successes may be missed and the overall impact of the advocacy effort may be underestimated. Bohan-Baker (2001) notes, on the other hand, that when evaluators focus only on process indicators, such as how many times a radio spot aired or how many pamphlets were distributed, without really addressing the outcomes of the project, such as how many people signed up for a service or whether the campaign re-framed public discussion of the problem, supporters will not be able to fully articulate what their advocacy efforts have accomplished. This calls for a more comprehensive approach to evaluation, including defining intermediate objectives to enable the evaluation team to demonstrate progress as the program continues working toward its longer-term goals (Bohan-Baker, 2001).

In order to measure outcomes, the specific goals of the advocacy effort must be clearly stated. While this may seem self-evident, overly general goals and objectives without measurable indicators are frequently encountered. Bohan-Baker (2001: 3) emphasizes the importance of clarity of advocacy goals when identifying evaluation indicators for a mass media campaign, noting that the

> critical question to ask is whether the mass media initiative is designed to make great shifts in public opinion on an issue or merely get the issue on the public agenda, providing information to encourage new ways to think about the issue. Which path the initiative chooses—moving public opinion or informing an audience—has significant implications for the specific goals, objectives and outcomes that are articulated early on, and therefore, what outcomes are ultimately measured.

As organizations become more involved with strategic communications activities, they will also need to develop the capacity to evaluate those activities. Stringer (1996) advises that people explore and reflect on the processes in which they have been engaging and to share perceptions and interpretations in order to gain greater clarity about the direction and efficacy of their work. This chapter will provide basic definitions of evaluation and examples of evaluated community advocacy projects as a means to encourage the reader to think of evaluation as a powerful tool for telling the "story" of what the advocacy efforts achieved, and the means by which those achievements were reached.

THE EVALUATION FRAMEWORK

Types of Evaluation

There are different types of evaluation, and differences among evaluators regarding how many types of evaluation there are, as well as the definition of each type. This chapter will follow the four types identified in the *Making Health Communication Programs Work* planning guide produced by the U.S. Department of Health and Human Services (1992). Each type of evaluation is designed to accomplish a specific task, such as to measure the results of a program, predict what those results might be, or examine why the results occurred. A well-designed evaluation will clearly describe each type of evaluation and the methods to be employed for data collection. It is important to remember that not all types of evaluation will be appropriate for every program, for example, an impact evaluation would not be appropriate for a one-year pilot program. The evaluation types include the following.

Formative Evaluation

Also known as formative research, this evaluation activity is conducted primarily at the start of the program, and includes all research which helps to inform the development of the intervention. Formative evaluation can also be part of the program monitoring process in some instances. For example, literature reviews, ethnographic investigations, pre-testing materials or messages, or preliminary assessments of target population knowledge of the problem to be addressed are all methods through which formative evaluation can be conducted.

Process Evaluation

The focus of a process evaluation is to examine the procedures and tasks involved in implementing a program. Process evaluation can answer questions about the types and quantities of services delivered, the beneficiaries of the services, resources used, and problems encountered, but not whether the program is having an impact on health behaviors or health status. For example, counting the number of community presentations, the number of telephone calls fielded, the number of hits to a website, or the number of people who received services are all examples of possible process evaluation indicators.

Outcome Evaluation

Outcome evaluation should provide information about the value of the program, rather than the quantity (process evaluation) and the achievement of short-term objectives. For example, outcome indicators might include the immediate effects of the program on the target populations such as changes in knowledge and attitudes (pre- and post-intervention surveys), expressed intent to change (surveys or interviews), behavior changes (surveys or analysis of changes in product purchases) and policy or institutional changes.

Impact Evaluation

This level of evaluation focuses on long-term changes resulting from the program, and is therefore the most comprehensive of the four types of evaluation. It can be difficult and costly to carry out an impact evaluation since it is typically conducted over longer periods of time, and direct attribution of the results to the program may be affected by external factors. Impact evaluation may look at changes in health status, changes in mortality, long-term maintenance of a behavior, recidivism, or broader policy changes. Some researchers call this "summative" evaluation.

Some researchers consider the terms "outcome" and "impact" to be synonyms, while others use the two terms in reverse order, that is, an "impact" evaluation would be what is defined in this chapter as outcome evaluation, and an "outcome" evaluation is what is defined here as "impact" evaluation. The important issue is that the program staff or evaluator clearly define what is meant by each type of evaluation proposed.

Types of Evaluation Data

Not only are there different types of evaluation, but there are also different types of data one can collect. The type of data collected will depend upon the program as well as the type(s) of evaluation. Analytic methods will depend upon the type of data collected. Types of evaluation data include the following.

Qualitative Data

Not to be confused with qualitative research, qualitative data are non-numerical observations systematically collected through established social science methods such as interviews, observational studies, narratives or case studies. In epidemiology, qualitative data refer to data which are categorical, non-numeric variables such as sex, disease status (e.g., yes [presence of disease]/no [absence of disease]), ethnicity, or place of birth.

Quantitative Data

Quantitative data are numeric variables which are either discrete or continuous, such as number of community presentations per week, number of radio spots aired, blood pressure, or age.

Evaluation Paradigms

All evaluation designs have a theoretical basis, which leads to the selection of specific design elements such as randomized control models, logic models, participatory evaluation, to name a few. Each approach to evaluation has strengths and weaknesses, and therefore the goals of the project must be clearly stated such that the evaluation framework is appropriate for the question(s) being asked. Conventional evaluations, also known as the "experimental approach" (Stecher and Davis, 1987) or "scientific method" (W.K. Kellogg Foundation, 1998), are based upon the generation of hypotheses which are then tested using statistical analysis techniques. The goal is to identify causal relationships between outcomes and the intervention designed to affect those outcomes. While some researchers see a randomized control model as the gold standard for assessing cause and effect, this may not in fact be appropriate for each setting. For example, conventional research methods which focus on program outcomes do not explain how or why programs are successful or under what circumstances they are successful (W.K. Kellogg Foundation, 1998). In multi-component community-based programs, such as community advocacy, the evaluation framework must be flexible enough to incorporate process and outcome evaluation in order to more fully understand the success or failure of a program.

The W.K. Kellogg Foundation *Evaluation Handbook* (1998) provides four alternative evaluation paradigms as examples to encourage those evaluating programs to consider other evaluation frameworks. The four examples are listed here so that readers of this chapter will also be stimulated to think more broadly about evaluation paradigms, the strengths and weaknesses of each paradigm, and how to effectively use evaluation to provide useful and relevant information to stakeholders.

Interpretivism/Constructivism

This paradigm focuses on understanding what is taking place in the program, rather than explaining results. It is based in anthropology, and relies heavily on qualitative research methods to develop an understanding of what the program means to those involved in it. According to the *Evaluation Handbook* (1998: 10), this paradigm allows for a holistic view of the program, something which is "often lost in conventional evaluations which rely on evaluator-determined categories of data collection, and do not focus on contextual factors." Grbich (1999: 30) describes interpretativist positions as "theory/concept-generating research" in her description of theoretical approaches to qualitative health research. Theory/concept-generating researchers examine the issue or question at hand without "overdirection," which might influence the data analysis and interpretation.

Feminist Methods

Feminist and other researchers with a specific ethnic or cultural perspective advocate for changes in conventional evaluation paradigms, as the experiences of women and minority groups have historically been omitted or ignored because those experiences did not fit into existing paradigms. Interpretations as to what constitutes feminist methods are quite diverse (W.W. Kellogg Foundation, 1998; Grbich, 1999). Grbich (1999) has enumerated the principles that have become associated with a feminist paradigm as being: a focus on the social construct of gender; acceptance of women as oppressed; a non-exploitative relationship between the researcher and the participants; a discussion of the researcher's values and how these are managed in the analysis and interpretation processes; and a focus on issues of power, honesty and ownership in the results.

Participatory Evaluation

This evaluation paradigm emphasizes the creation of an understanding of the program and of program impacts from the perspective of the multiple stakeholders of the program. This paradigm is called the "responsive evaluation approach" by Stecher and Davis (1987). Responsive evaluation seeks to understand the issue from the perspectives of all program stakeholders, based on the assumption that no single answer to a program question exists that can be found by using tests, questionnaires, or statistical analyses. The W.K. Kellogg Foundation *Evaluation Handbook* (1998) describes participatory evaluation as one where the perspectives of the program participants and stakeholders are given equal weight or value as that of the evaluator's perspective, and that actively engages all the stakeholders in the evaluation process. The focus of participatory evaluation is to provide results that are useful and relevant to the program stakeholders.

Theory-Based Evaluation

This approach developed from attempts to evaluate comprehensive community-based initiatives that do not lend themselves to a statistical analysis of outcomes (W.K. Kellogg Foundation, 1998). This approach assumes that every program is based upon an explicit or implicit theory, or process, which describes how and why the program will work. For this evaluation paradigm, it is necessary to identify the theory or process in order to successfully understand what the key program elements are. This program model, also known as a logic model, should describe how the program works by linking outcomes with program activities. As described in the *Evaluation Handbook* (1998: 35), a program logic model is a "picture of how the program works."

MEDIA ADVOCACY

Monitoring media content is a basic element of evaluating media advocacy. This monitoring includes simple counts of newspaper articles or television or radio coverage on the problem being addressed through the advocacy efforts. The first step in counting, however, is to define all the possible subject areas which might be related to the advocacy topic and which can be used to code the media coverage for future analysis. For example, if the advocacy efforts are to increase community and political support for a clean syringe exchange program, possible subject areas under which articles or news commentaries could appear might be clean syringe exchange programs, drug abuse, drug treatment, HIV or hepatitis C infection (HCV), living with AIDS, criminal justice policies to reduce drug use, or substance abuse. Treno and Holder (1997b) advocate for the use of both structured (e.g., forms on which intervention activities or events are recorded) and unstructured (e.g., narrative reports, interviews) community monitoring tools to better evaluate results of community mobilization and media advocacy activities. Their article describes in detail how this was conducted for the Community Trials Project, a community mobilization and media advocacy program to reduce alcohol-related trauma.

Once the subject areas for a media advocacy evaluation have been identified, articles or television news coverage pieces should be categorized by the type of coverage (e.g., editorial, feature, news) and each media piece coded by content (Treno and Holder, 1997b). A content analysis can be conducted to assess how the media are covering the issue and whether the advocacy effort has been successful in reframing the issue consistent with goals of the advocacy efforts (Bohan-Baker, 2001). Content analysis and measuring the size of the print article or tracking the number of minutes dedicated to the topic on television coverage can help assess whether advocacy efforts have been successful in generating media attention and increased the level of reporting on the issue. (Treno and Holder, 1997b).

According to Bernard (1994), the term "content analysis" covers a variety of techniques for making inferences from text data. The goal of content analysis is to reduce large amounts of data into categories; these categories can then be used in either quantitative (e.g., counting the number of times the category appears) or qualitative (e.g., a comparison of categories across time or other program relevant variables) studies. The construction of the codes for content analysis is critical to both the reliability and validity of the research; if one person is responsible for developing the codes, then construct validity may be compromised, however even when codes are developed by a group of people reliability may be affected if only one person is responsible for doing the coding (Bernard, 1994). Ways to reduce these problems include development of codes by more than one person, rigorous training of coders, use of multiple coders, and an assessment of intercoder reliability.

Challenges with content analysis of media coverage of the advocacy efforts are also noted by Treno and Holder (1997b). These include coverage which did not necessarily reflect the community mobilization efforts due to a preference by the media to cover events rather than issues (e.g., car crashes rather than the issue of driving under the influence [DUI]), coding reliability over time, and differences in media consumption habits by population groups. The authors note that monitoring media coverage can help program staff to more successfully target media attention, for example, using DUI checkpoints to highlight the issue of drinking and driving.

In the case of the Community Trials Project, a process evaluation focusing on the number of meetings or attendance at meetings would not have provided the program with the type of information needed to determine whether the goal of community mobilization was achieved. Treno and Holder (1997b) identified three elements which needed to be in place in order for the community mobilization to be deemed successful: (1) high local news attention to the prevention strategies and problems being addressed (alcohol-related trauma in communities), (2) high community and opinion leader support for the interventions being proposed (changes in policy regarding server training, alcohol billboard restrictions, reduction in alcohol availability, loss of driver's license for first-time DUI, and DUI spot checkpoints), and (3) at least a minimum-level implementation of the interventions.

The authors used both qualitative and quantitative data to assess progress in each area, including narrative summary of the content analysis, counts of the subject areas covered in the print and television news and community surveys pre- and post-implementation of the mobilization efforts. However, they found that although there were differences in media consumption habits by income and educational level of the community residents, most community members were concerned about alcohol problems among youth and drinking-and-driving accidents. However, they found less support among the residents for the interventions to reduce alcohol-related trauma, although those interventions which appeared to be most targeted to the problem behavior, such as mandatory server training, and the loss of a driver's license for first-time drunk drivers, did receive general support.

COMMUNITY-WIDE INTERVENTIONS

Mothers Against Drunk Driving

Mothers Against Drunk Driving (MADD) may be one of the most recognized grassroots organizations in the country. Founded in 1980 by a group of mothers after the death of a young teenager hit by a repeat offender drunk driver, the organization twenty years later has 600 chapters nationwide with over three million members (MADD, 2002). A review of the literature revealed more published studies on MADD than any other national grassroots organization, although evaluation-related studies tended to focus on a specific activity or one aspect of the organization's structure. Bloch and Ungerleider (1988) examined apparent discrepancies within the organization's programmatic (prevention emphasis) and legislative (punitive emphasis) efforts. These discrepancies have arisen, in part, due to well-publicized successes of MADD's advocacy efforts in the legislative arena and relatively little media attention on other MADD activities. The successes of the organization on many levels, including expansion of MADD chapters throughout the country (from 2 chapters in 1980 to 400 by 1986, and over 600 in 2002) and significant accomplishments in the legislative arena (e.g., the first Presidential Commission to study drinking and driving in 1982 and enactment of over 300 drunken driving laws by 1986), have earned the organization a national reputation for its advocacy efforts (Bloch and Ungerleider, 1988).

The Organizational Mission

Given the obvious positive outcomes of MADD, why should it be necessary to conduct a formal evaluation of its advocacy efforts and the ways in which the organization carries out its mission? Bloch and Ungerleider

(1988) note that a well-designed evaluation can serve as a guide to other similar agencies as they undertake advocacy efforts, or as they establish new chapters. The authors examined the differences between the media image of the national organization and the operation of local chapters. The authors used a survey design to determine whether MADD was a "retributive organization," as some researchers claimed, and whether the focus of the organization's advocacy efforts was purely punitive. The authors mailed surveys to the leaders of all viable chapters nationwide in 1986 to assess the "victimization status" of chapter leaders and members (whether the individual or their family or friends had been a victim of an alcohol-related accident) and how this may influence local chapter activities, types of chapter activities, chapter resources, and deterrence approaches that chapter leaders felt were effective in solving the drinking and driving problem.

Bloch and Ungerleider rejected assertions that MADD is a retributive organization and that the focus of the organization is solely punitive, that is, promoting punishment of drunk drivers. The authors found that three of MADD's four most emphasized programs across a wide range of chapters focused on information dissemination, such as speakers' bureaus and school programs that are intended to prevent drunk driving. The authors did note a disparity in the survey results, in that MADD chapter leaders supported and engaged in prevention programming, although they tended to view criminal justice-type programs as being more effective deterrents to drinking and driving. The authors hypothesized that this may be a result of a shift in ideological orientation from prevention to criminal justice, with programmatic components reflecting the earlier focus. Alternatively, leaders may support prevention programs, despite their own conviction that punishment is the greater deterrent, because of community or donor support of those programs.

Media Advocacy

Other researchers have examined the effectiveness of specific MADD advocacy efforts, including media advocacy activities. Russell and colleagues (1995) evaluated a media advocacy event organized around the release of the 1993 "Rating the States Report," a report-card on the nation's fight against alcohol-impaired driving. The authors examined how MADD organized the media advocacy efforts and the results of those efforts, and provide guidelines for advocacy groups using media advocacy to promote their mission. The authors defined media advocacy as "an effort to move public discourse from a focus on individual blame to a more proper focus on societal conditions and institutional arrangements that are at the root of the public health problem" (Russell, Voas, DeJong, and Chaloupka, 1995: 240). Since media advocacy is a major focus of MADD, it is useful to examine why its media advocacy has been so successful over the lifetime of the organization.

In the early 1990s, MADD and Advocates for Highway and Auto Safety developed the "Rating the States" Program. Indicators reflecting each state's commitment to reduce alcohol-impaired driving were developed by a panel of experts and states were scored on each indicator (Russell et al., 1995). The two organizations issued the second report in 1993. The production of such a report card would have been difficult for a governmental agency because of political ramifications; a national grassroots organization with both the capacity and moral authority to use the data, such as MADD, was the appropriate sponsor. MADD leaders followed up in person with state government leaders to ensure that the data for each indicator were provided as fully as possible. Scores for each state were translated into one grade ranging from "A" to "D." The two organizations released the report at a press conference in Washington, D.C., with local press conferences organized by MADD chapters just before the Thanksgiving holiday, when people throughout the United States travel. The release of the report generated significant national media coverage, both on television and in print; audio news releases also generated additional radio coverage. Process evaluation documented the number of news stories that resulted, the types of programs that featured the stories, and the number of local stations which produced their own news segment. Using the process indicators, the authors estimated that an audience of 62.5 million people was reached by broadcast and newspaper and an additional 1.2 million were reached by radio (Russell, et al. 1995). Outcome indicators for the impact of the report and the media advocacy campaign included actions which took place at the state level after the release of the report, e.g., the Governor of Alabama appointed a special task force on alcohol-impaired driving four months after release of the report, which reflected unfavorably on the state; a constitutional amendment for victim rights was passed by the Idaho state legislature, which also received a poor grade in the report; Michigan organized a statewide forum on alcohol issues with MADD as a participant.

Russell and colleagues (1995) then developed 18 recommendations for organizations considering media advocacy based upon MADD's experience in developing the Rating the States report and the media advocacy campaign that accompanied its release. Through the evaluation, the authors also identified five key program elements that should be in place for media advocacy to be successful. First, the organization must be credible and have widespread public recognition and support. In the case of MADD, the organization also speaks with moral authority because its membership consists primarily of people who have been affected by alcohol-impaired driving. Second, data should be collected in such a way to permit people to compare their local jurisdiction to other areas, e.g., by state in this case, or by county for a statewide campaign. Third, data should be presented in an easy-to-understand format; in this example, most people immediately understood the meaning of the letter grade. Fourth, indicators must reflect actions of governmental or community leaders so that there can be specific calls to action, which will also attract the news media. Finally, the program should involve professional companies specializing in public relations or media events if the organization lacks the expertise.

Community Coalitions/Community Mobilizing

A limited number of studies evaluating the impact of community coalitions or community mobilization efforts is available (Berkowitz, 2001). Berkowitz (2001) notes in his summary of research on community coalitions that there are few published outcome studies in general, and even fewer with empirically collected outcome data. A challenge noted by Berkowitz is that common definitions have not yet been established for the terms "coalition," "collaborative," or "community initiative," leading to problems in comparing programs across these different forms of "community-based cooperative activities." The author defines community coalitions as (1) having representation from a number of community sectors, (2) paying attention to multiple community issues, (3) engendering active community participation, and (4) conducting planning and decisionmaking from the bottom up. In contrast, community collaboratives are often agency-driven or focus on a single issue, or both, while community initiatives are agency-driven and often focus on economic development or housing (Berkowitz, 2001).

While evidence for positive outcomes is reported to be rare (Kreuter et al., 2000, cited in Berkowitz, 2001; Roussos and Fawcett, 2000), some authors have noted that the lack of evidence of positive outcomes resulting from community-wide initiatives may be a result of inappropriate research models and ill-defined key elements and methods for implementing the initiative (Cummings, 1999). In his review of community-based tobacco control initiatives, Cummings (1999) notes that use of a traditional randomized control model may not be appropriate for the evaluation of large-scale community changes. The author remarks on the "dynamic nature" of such community interventions, and suggests that time-series designs may be more applicable for the evaluation of community-based interventions.

A Healthier Diet: Public Relations and Low-Fat Milk

Reger, Wootan and Booth-Butterfield (2000) compared the effectiveness of two education approaches to encourage consumers to switch from high-fat (whole or 2%) to low-fat (1% or fat-free) milk as part of a healthy lifestyles campaign. One community received a public relations campaign and community-based educational activities, such as training of community volunteers to give community presentations and conduct outreach to schools and churches; milk tasting sessions at supermarkets, schools and other community locations; and a press conference at the start and close of the campaign. The second community received a paid advertising campaign, while the third community served as the comparison community. The authors conducted pre-and post-intervention surveys and examined milk sales at supermarkets located in the three towns pre-intervention and at two post-intervention timepoints: immediately and six-months after the campaign concluded.

As a result of the interventions, self-reported change from high to low-fat milk was significant in the two intervention communities, with no change noted for the comparison community. However, in the community with the combined public relations and community activities, sales of low-fat milk increased from 23% to 28% (p = n.s.) between baseline and immediate post-intervention, and remained at that level six months post-campaign. For the community that received only paid advertising, sales of low-fat milk increased from 28% to 34% (p = n.s.), but returned to baseline six months later. The authors hypothesized that with community members continually exposed to advertisements, well-designed public relations activities can attract news coverage and provide a means for reinforcing other program components which the paid advertising cannot.

The use of public relations and community-based activities reported by Reger and colleagues (2000) reflects the experience reported by Wechsler and Wernick (1992) and Wechsler, Basch, Zybert and Shea (1998), in which a community-based cardiovascular disease prevention program included public relations activities in addition to traditional health education methods and social marketing. A summary of the evaluation of the multifaceted six-year healthy heart program reported a documented increase in consumer demand for low-fat (1%) milk and policy changes resulting in increased availability of low-fat milk from 6 to 20 of a total of 28 institutions serving children in the target area (Shea, Basch, Wechsler, and Lantigua, 1996). The authors also noted that "vigorous advocacy" for continued

financial support of the program from the State of New York, the original
funder, was necessary, and additional funding was obtained as a result.

Community Trials Project and Alcohol-Related Trauma

Treno and Holder (1997a) report on the evaluation of the community
mobilization component of the Community Trials Project, a 15-site project
to assess the implementation of community-level alcohol policies that have
the potential to reduce alcohol-related trauma. The authors (1997b: 166)
define community mobilization as "the activation of the community (local
organizations, leaders, community members) in support of a specific [local
problem]." Because community mobilization is a process by which an objective is achieved, the authors note that a process evaluation is therefore required, but that mobilization efforts also need to be evaluated by
their contribution to the implementation of the interventions that will
actually resolve the local problem. In the Community Trials Project, mobilization included community organizing and media advocacy. The authors used weekly project summary reports, which included the number
and description of activities conducted, and interviewed project coordina-
tors to evaluate the level and extent of community mobilization in three
of the Community Trials Project sites. Treno and Holder (1997a) report
that the overall goal of policy implementation was achieved at each of the
three sites, and highlight elements which supported the organization of
the community coalitions and the achievement of goals.

Wagenaar and colleagues (2000) report on a 15-site Community Trials
Project undertaken in the Midwestern region of the United States. The
Communities Mobilizing for Change on Alcohol (CMCA), a randomized
community trial design in which communities were randomly assigned to
either the intervention or control group, was designed to reduce the acc-
essibility of alcoholic beverages to youths under the legal drinking age.
In addition to a baseline and three-year post-intervention survey design
(e.g., reported drinking behaviors), the project also included a multiple
time-series design so that some outcome variables, such as access to alcohol from commercial and social sources, were measured more frequently
both pre- and during intervention implementation. To evaluate the impact
of the mobilization efforts, the authors conducted school-based surveys,
telephone surveys of 18- to 20-year-olds, alcohol purchase attempts by
youth who appeared to be underage, and telephone interviews of owners
and managers of alcohol outlets. The authors report that the community
organizing intervention significantly and favorably affected the behavior
of 18- to 20-year-olds and on-site alcohol establishments (bars, restaurants);

18-to-20 year-olds reduced their reported purchases of alcohol for under-age youth, were less likely to try to purchase alcohol, reported increased difficulty in purchasing alcohol, and were less likely to have had a drink in the past 30-day period. While both on- and off-site (liquor stores, gro-cery stores) alcohol establishments increased age-identification checks and reported reducing sales of alcohol to minors, on-site establishments had higher levels of positive changes. The only area where no changes were seen across the outcome variables was with seniors in high school. The re-searchers (2000) concluded from their results that community organizing and mobilization can result in community institutional and policy changes.

EVALUATING SYRINGE EXCHANGE
ADVOCACY EFFORTS

In San Diego County, elected officials have justified their failure to approve the implementation of a clean syringe exchange program for the prevention of ongoing transmission of blood-borne pathogens among in-jection drug users, their syringe-sharing partners, and their sexual partners by stating that the general public does not support clean syringe exchange and by claiming that published evaluation studies were inconclusive. The question of the quality of evaluation results of other clean syringe ex-change programs raised by elected officials was addressed by reviewing the literature on a regular basis, direct contact with researchers involved in syringe exchange program evaluation and provision of summaries of the literature by well recognized sources (e.g., the Surgeon General, the Centers for Disease Control and Prevention) to elected officials. This in-depth understanding of evaluation methods and results enabled the team conducting outreach to elected officials to effectively address concerns dur-ing presentations or provide the information within 24- to 48-hours of the meeting.

As elected officials could not justify statements regarding clean syringe exchange evaluation data, greater reliance was placed on the statement "the community will not support this." In 1998, Alliance Healthcare Foundation undertook a Public Education and Advocacy Campaign for Clean Syringe Exchange in San Diego County to educate the general public and elected officials in particular, about the true cost of continued transmission of hep-atitis C and HIV among San Diego County residents. A conscious decision was made to focus on the disease risks and unintended consequences of the public disposal of used syringes to the general public, rather than on the needs of injection drug users. This decision was based on a review of the foundation's 1994 through 1997 advocacy efforts on clean syringe exchange, which indicated little impact on local decision-makers or community leaders. Individuals experienced in working with elected officials, such as public relations experts, lobbyists and former staff to elected officials, were hired to help focus the messages for the 1998 campaign. One positive result of the 1994–1997 advocacy efforts was a public opinion poll conducted by a San Diego research organization, indicating high levels of community support for a clean syringe exchange program if the program were part of a comprehensive HIV prevention effort and injection drug users would have access to drug treatment resources. The survey results were used to inform the general population that clean syringe exchange as part of a continuum of prevention services did have broader acceptance.

Phase I of the Public Education and Advocacy Campaign focused on creating a public discourse on the issue of ongoing preventable disease transmission among San Diego County residents, and the identification of available options to reduce the risk of infection. Since the first phase of the campaign also coincided with an election year for both city and county officials, the advocacy team worked to frame the issue as one that candidates running for office would have to address. The evaluation plan included formative, process and outcome evaluations. Focus groups with diverse groups of residents were conducted as part of the formative evaluation to determine what people needed to know in order to make a decision to support clean syringe exchange; whether there were differences in acceptance of the messages by ethnicity, gender or age group; reliable sources of information on health issues; and identification of important local community leaders to involve in the advocacy campaign. In addition, a small-scale pre-test of the print materials was conducted and materials were modified as needed.

Process evaluation consisted of tracking the number of community presentations; individual presentations to elected officials; individual presentations to candidates running for office; information packets on clean syringe exchange distributed; visits to the foundation's website over the course of the campaign; op-ed pieces printed in the leading local newspaper; letters-to-the-editor; articles in the newspaper on HIV, hepatitis C, injection drug use and treatment options for substance abusers; television and radio interviews of campaign spokespersons; and campaign staff participation in radio call-in shows.

Evaluation of Phase I activities revealed that the formative evaluation had been critical for the development of messages which resonated with voters; tracking of "negative" versus "positive" calls and e-mail messages to the foundation indicated that most were supportive of clean syringe exchange as part of a comprehensive hepatitis C and HIV prevention program, and hits to the foundation web site increased after airing each of the three radio spots. In addition, participation in two radio call-in shows which targeted very different listener groups (one a conservative audience and one a moderate to liberal audience) resulted in more calls from supporters than opponents on both shows.

Outcome indicators for Phase 1 of the campaign included positioning clean syringe exchange as a campaign issue and identification of elected officials willing to introduce clean syringe exchange for discussion at the city or county administrative level. Both outcomes were achieved, with mayoral candidates participating in a community forum asked to explain their position on syringe exchange by a member of the audience not associated with the campaign. The most important outcome from Phase 1 was the decision of a key San Diego city council member to bring the issue to the Public Services and Neighborhood Safety Committee of the City of San Diego City Council. Using these results, the foundation launched Phase II of the campaign.

Phase II of the Public Education and Advocacy Campaign for Clean Syringe Exchange specifically targeted City of San Diego elected officials and local community leaders, in particular religious and business leaders. Advocacy activities were focused on one-to-one meetings with elected officials, community leaders, religious groups, religious leaders, business groups (e.g., the San Diego Chamber of Commerce) and business leaders (e.g., CEOs of large corporations).

Outcome evaluation was the focus for the evaluation of Phase 2 given the highly targeted nature of the advocacy efforts. Two indicators were identified as indicators of success, with a positive outcome needed for each one: the declaration of a medical state of emergency by the San Diego City Council and approval of a pilot clean syringe exchange program as part of the medical state of emergency.

DISCUSSION QUESTIONS

1.   You are the coordinator of a large-scale community advocacy program to change public policies which currently limit supportive services for foster youth aging out of the foster care system. These policies make it difficult for agencies to continue to provide services to foster youth once they reach 18 years of age, although many of the young people need continued assistance in order to become self-sufficient adults. Describe how would you evaluate the program and what appropriate process and outcome indicators for the evaluation of the program activities would be.

2. You are a member of a neighborhood association that has identified speeding in residential neighborhoods as a priority action item due to several recent accidents involving speeding vehicles and pedestrians. What would be an appropriate evaluation paradigm, and how would you evaluate success or failure of the association to resolve the problem of speeding drivers?

REFERENCES

Berkowitz, B. (2001). Studying the outcomes of community-based coalitions. *American Journal of Community Psychology, 29*, 213–227.

Bernard, H.R. (1994). *Research Methods in Anthropology: Qualitative and Quantitative Approaches*. Thousand Oaks, CA: Sage.

Bloch S., Ungerleider S. (1988). Whither the drunk driving movement? The social and programmatic orientations of Mothers Against Drunk Driving. *Evaluation and Program Planning, 11*, 237–244.

Bohan-Baker, M. (2001). Theory and practice: Pitching policy change. *The Evaluation Exchange Newsletter, 7*, Harvard Family Research Project. http://gseweb.harvard.edu/~hfrp/eval/issue16.

Cummings, K.M. (1999). Community-wide interventions for tobacco control. *Nicotine & Tobacco Research, Supplement 1*, S111–112.

Grbich, C. (1999). *Qualitative Research in Health: An Introduction*. Thousand Oaks, CA: Sage Publications.

MADD (2002). Irving, Texas (January 20, 2002); http://www.madd.org.

Reger, B., Wootan, M.G., Booth-Butterfield, S. (2000). A comparison of different approaches to promote community-wide dietary change. *American Journal of Preventive Medicine, 18*, 271–275.

Roussos, S.T., Fawcett, S.B. (2000). A review of collaborative partnerships as a strategy for improving community health. *Annual Review of Public Health, 21*, 369–402.

Russell, A., Voas, R.B., DeJong, W., Chaloupka, M. (1995). MADD rates the states: A media advocacy event to advance the agenda against alcohol-impaired driving. *Public Health Reports, 110*, 240–245.

Shea, S., Basch, C.E., Wechsler, H., Lantigua, R. (1996). The Washington Heights-Inwood Healthy Heart Program: A six-year report from a disadvantaged urban setting. *American Journal of Public Health, 86*, 166–171.

Stecher, B.M., Davis, W.A. (1987). *How to Focus an Evaluation*. Newbury Park, CA: Sage.

Stringer, E.T. (1996). *Action Research: A Handbook for Practitioners*. Thousand Oaks, CA: Sage.

Treno, A.J., Holder, H.D. (1997a). Community mobilization: evaluation of an environmental approach to local action. *Addiction, 92*, S173–S187.

Treno, A.J., Holder, H.D. (1997b). Community mobilization, organizing, and media advocacy. A discussion of methodological issues. *Evaluation Review, 21*, 166–190.

United States Department of Health and Human Services (1992). *Making Health Communication Programs Work: A Planner's Guide*. Office of Cancer Communications, National Cancer Institute, National Institutes of Health, Bethesda, MD. NIH Publication Number 92-1493.

Wagenaar, A.C., Murray, D.M., Gehan, J.P., Wolfson, M., Forster, J.L., Toomey, T.L., Perry, C.L., Jones-Webb, R. (2000). Communities Mobilizing for Change on Alcohol:

Outcomes from a Randomized Community Trial. *Journal of Studies on Alcohol, 61,* 85–94.

Wechsler, H., Basch, C.E., Zybert, P., Shea, S. (1998). Promoting the selection of low-fat milk in elementary school cafeterias in an inner-city Latino community: Evaluation of an intervention. *American Journal of Public Health, 88,* 427–432.

Wechsler, H., Wernick, S.M. (1992). A social marketing campaign to promote low-fat milk consumption in an inner-city Latino community. *Public Health Reports, 107,* 202–207.

Weiss, H.B. (2001). Strategic Communications. *The Evaluation Exchange Newsletter, 7,* Harvard Family Research Project. http://gseweb.harvard.edu/~hfrp/eval/issue16.

W.K. Kellogg Foundation (1998). *Evaluation Handbook.* Battle Creek, MI.

Woodruff, K. (1996). Alcohol advertising and violence against women: A media advocacy case study. *Health Education Quarterly, 23,* 330–345.

CHAPTER TEN

Advocacy and Ethics

> 'Tis not the many oaths that makes the truth,
> But the plain single vow that is vowed true.
> William Shakespeare, *All's Well That Ends Well*, IV, ii, 21

ADVOCACY AND ETHICS: ARE THE TWO COMPATIBLE?

As we have seen in the previous chapters, an advocacy role can take many forms, such as conducting a needs assessment and publicizing the findings, participation in grassroots organizing efforts, responding to a published proposed regulation, and assisting a legislator's office with the drafting of a new bill. The appropriateness of health researchers engaging in such activities has come under attack, however. (Research as a component of advocacy efforts is addressed in chapters 2 and 3.) For instance, Rothman and Poole (1985) have asserted that a researcher's participation in public advocacy is inappropriate; participation in the advocacy process is appropriate only if the researcher is acting in his or her role as a private citizen (Poole and Rothman, 1990). By contrast, Weed (1994) has justified an advocacy role for epidemiologists by focusing on the principle of beneficence which, stated somewhat simplistically, centers on the obligation to do good (Beauchamp and Childress, 1994). Bankowski (1991:162) has spoken to the positive role that epidemiologists as researchers can play; his comments are applicable, as well, to other health professionals:

> Epidemiology is a means of quantifying injustice in relation to health care, of monitoring progress towards justice, beneficence, non-maleficence, and respect for persons, as these ethical principles apply to society, and of applying

its findings to the control of health problems. That those at the political level charged with safeguarding the public health often neglect or find it inconvenient, or even impractical, to apply epidemiological findings, sometimes because the more vulnerable populations or groups lack the power to assert or safeguard their rights, often because of the complexity of prioritizing resources allocation, does not invalidate epidemiology. Rather, that this happens is a reason for emphasizing the relation between ethics and human values and health policy-making, and for an ethics of public health, concerned with social justice as well as individual rights, to complement the ethics of medicine.

Gordis (1991: 12S) envisions the epidemiologist assuming a societal role in the policy-making process through the presentation of data and its interpretations and the development and evaluation of proposals. He acknowledges, however, that a researcher's credibility may be lessened if he or she assumes a strong advocacy position on a specific issue:

> An additional consideration is that since our data have important societal implications, if we want society to continue to support our efforts, we will have to demonstrate the value of our research for the health of the public. This can only be done if we broaden our responsibility from the research only role to that of policy-related functions. Thus, the epidemiologist must also serve as an educator. Her efforts are directed at many target populations including other scientists, legislators, policy makers, lawyers and judges, and the public. Each must be dealt with differently depending on the specific needs of that population and the objectives towards which the educational effort is directed.

Ultimately, each health professional will have to decide for him- or herself the advisability of engaging in advocacy efforts and the extent to which he or she will do so.

DEFINING COMMUNITY

Even how we define community in a given circumstance may present ethical issues requiring resolution. We know from chapter 1 that "community" may be defined geographically, based on a specific issue of interest, based on membership in a particular organization or as a function of having a specified disease. Ultimately, our definition of community indicates who is to be included and who is to be excluded; this, in turn, may reflect our notions of justice (Rawls, 1971).

Consider, for example, the advocacy efforts to end AIDS discrimination, detailed in chapter 7. Individuals brought lawsuits to end discrimination in schools, in places of employment, in the receipt of medical care because they were excluded from the public's definition of community: AIDS-diagnosed individuals were "them," distinct from "us," because they had a dreaded disease. These lawsuits would have been unnecessary, and related legislation would have been unnecessary if, in the communities in which individuals worked, played, lived, and studied, there had been a "sense of community" that had included individuals with HIV infection. Rather, HIV-infected individuals became a community defined by their medical status; their friends and families became members of that same community by association.

COMMUNITY CONSENT

The issue of community consent is related to the precepts of "starting where the people are," and of community readiness, which were discussed in detail in conjunction with grassroots advocacy efforts in chapter 3.

On an individual level, consent to participate in a health procedure or health study requires that the prospective participant be given the necessary facts about what is to happen, that he or she understand those facts, that he or she have the capacity to consent to participate, and that the consent, when given, is voluntary (Beauchamp and Childress, 1994). The application of these principles at the community level may require some creativity.

Consider, for instance, the case study involving the San Diego needle exchange program, detailed in chapters 1 and 9. Elected officials had claimed that the community would never accept a needle exchange program. If this were true, the implementation of a needle exchange program could fail miserably due to numerous potential barriers: the refusal of the police department to recognize the program's validity and the arrests of individuals as they made the exchanges; the refusal of neighborhoods to tolerate a needle exchange program in its vicinity; and the unwillingness of injection drug users to utilize the services of the programs for fear of arrest and further stigmatization. Clearly, some level of community consent, or "buy-in," was required to assure first, that the proposal would receive a positive vote from the City Council and, second, that once approved, the program would have the support of the community. This was accomplished by providing the community with information necessary to make an informed decision regarding the value of such a program and the involvement of a broad range of stakeholders in the advocacy efforts.

UNANTICIPATED CONSEQUENCES

Sometimes, the best of intentions may drive an advocacy effort, but that effort may result in unintended adverse consequences. In such instances, one must consider whether the advocacy effort has been consistent with the principles of beneficence, to do good, and that of nonmaleficence, to refrain from doing harm. Sometimes it may be difficult to determine whether an effort's consequences have resulted in good or in harm; the ultimate conclusion may well depend on one's perspective.

Consider, for example, the actions of ACT UP targeting the Catholic Church for its stance against the use of condoms, detailed in chapter 3. Some might view these actions as ultimately contributing to the ability of HIV-infected individuals to receive care and to prevention programs to receive funds, because the actions drew attention to the need for such funding. Others might dismiss the effort as ultimately having harmed advocacy efforts for HIV-infected individuals, arguing that the action was ineffectual—and that the organizers should have known from the beginning that it would be ineffectual—in moving the Church towards a more liberal policy on the use of condoms and that the Church has no authority with respect to access to care or to prevention services.

CONFLICTS OF INTEREST

Some might assume that a health professional who has assumed the role of advocate would not be challenged by ethical dilemmas. After all, isn't the person working for the good of the community? Isn't this goal to supercede all else?

In actuality, the health professional who is working, in some fashion, as an advocate, is often confronted with situations that demand attention to ethical considerations. For instance, the health educator may be torn by conflicting loyalties to a specific community and to his or her agency, whose agenda may not be congruent with the wishes of the community. In other situations, the health worker may face community reluctance to implement a particular strategy or to address a specific health problem and, as a result, may have to resort to more coercive measures, raising issues related to the informed consent of the community. In yet other cases, a health program may be implemented with the best of intentions in order to address a serious health issue, yet the long-term effects of the program may be deleterious, or the program may have even unintended adverse short-term consequences. These and similar issues are addressed below.

Defining Conflict of Interest

A conflict of interest in the context of epidemiology has been defined as occurring whenever a personal interest or a role obligation of an investigator conflicts with the obligation to uphold another party's interest, thereby compromising normal expectations of reasonable objectivity in regard to the other party. Such circumstances are almost always to be scrupulously avoided in conducting epidemiologic investigations.

Every epidemiologist has the potential for such conflict. An epidemiologist on the payroll of a corporation, a university, or a government does not encounter a conflict merely by the condition of employment, but a conflict exists whenever the epidemiologist's role obligation or personal interest in accommodating the institution, in job security, or in personal goals compromises obligations to others who have a right to expect objectivity and fairness. (Beauchamp et al., 1991:151S).

Despite its focus on epidemiologists, the definition is equally valid for other health professionals who are contemplating engaging in advocacy efforts. Consider, for example, the dilemma faced by the head of a local health department in the following scenario. (See references to needle exchange programs in Chapters 1–4 for details relating to such programs and actual advocacy efforts.)

Dr. X. is the head of a large county health department. A large proportion of the AIDS cases in the county are attributable to injection drug use. There are few available publicly-funded treatment slots for heroin-using injection drug users, and none for individuals who are injecting other drugs, such as cocaine or methamphetamine. There is no legal needle exchange program. Dr. X. is aware of the large body of scientific literature demonstrating the efficacy and effectiveness of needle exchange programs and was an outspoken advocate for such programs in his previous position, in another city. In his current position as head of public health, he is beholden to his employers, the members of the County Board of Supervisors, who have the power to fire him at will. The Board has indicated that, under no circumstances, will it ever approve the implementation of a needle exchange program, even on a pilot basis. Dr. X. is torn between his desire to advocate for a program that he is convinced will ultimately save lives and the realization that if he should do so, his efforts will ultimately fail due to lack of support from the Board of Supervisors and he will be relieved of his position.

The Source of Conflicts of Interest

A conflict of interest may stem from any of several motivating forces, including altruism, a desire for personal recognition, or the possibility of financial reward. Even when there is no actual conflict of interest, a perceived conflict of interest may result in the erosion of trust (Beauchamp et al., 1991) of the public. Consider, for example, the following hypothetical situation. (See chapter 7 for a discussion of advocacy through the courts in the context of domestic violence, which provides the basis for this hypothetical example.)

A psychologist has been called to testify in a case involving the attempted murder of a man by his wife. She has been the victim of spousal abuse for an extended period of time. She attempted to kill her husband with a large butcher knife as he lay sleeping. He had fallen asleep after having had an argument with his wife, which centered around her incompetence at preparing dinner, and after he had slammed her head into the kitchen wall, resulting in a bleeding wound on her forehead and a hole in the dry wall. Objectively, the psychologist believes that leaving the home would have been the best option for the wife, as there are emergency shelters in the community that would have had openings for her. However, she sympathizes with the woman's plight and does not believe that the potential jail sentence is justified in view of the many years of abuse that the woman has suffered. The psychologist is torn between giving an objective opinion, and giving one that is more reflective of her concern for the woman, since the lawyer is asking her only for her opinion, without specifying the nature of that opinion.

Consider a situation in which a coalition is to be formed to address a particular health issue. (See chapter 4 for a discussion of coalition development.) The original organizers of the advocacy effort must decide who is to be included as members of this coalition. This, in turn, requires that a judgment be made as to which individuals or organizations truly represent the interests of the stakeholder communities. Self-identified leaders may, or may not, actually represent the communities or the communities' interests that they claim; they may, in fact, be acting to serve their own political or financial interests.

DISCUSSION QUESTIONS

1. You are working for the county department of public health. The department has been particularly concerned with the recent increase in the number of individuals who are homeless and the health risks that accompany homelessness. The county commissioners have requested that the health department determine the prevalence of homelessness. Several entities have offered to assist with this effort, including a number of nonprofit organizations that work with homeless individuals, the Chamber of Commerce, and a number of religious groups. You have decided to form a coalition to provide guidance to this effort, and have invited these entities to send representatives to participate as members of the coalition. What possible conflicts of interest may exist and how might they affect the process? What ethical issues do they raise?

2. As a public health person, you have been concerned with the apparent unavailability of publicly-funded treatment slots for outpatient

substance abuse treatment. You have decided to conduct a needs assessment of the community to determine the extent of need for such services. Assume that you live in a large, metropolitan area with a diverse population. How will you define the community for the purpose of this needs assessment and who will you involve in the process? What ethical issues are raised in this process? By your decision?

REFERENCES

Bankowski, Z. (1991). Epidemiology, ethics, and 'health for all.' *Law, Medicine & Health Care, 19*, 162–163.

Beauchamp, T.L., Childress, J.F. (1994). *Principles of Biomedical Ethics*. New York: Oxford University Press.

Beauchamp, T.L., Cook, R.R., Fayerweather, W.E., Raabe, G.K., Thar, W.E., Cowles, S.R., Spivey, G.H. (1991). Ethical guidelines for epidemiologists. *Journal of Clinical Epidemiology, 44*, 151S–169S.

Gordis, L. (1991). Ethical and professional issues in the changing practice of epidemiology. *Journal of Clinical Epidemiology, 44*, 9S–13S.

Poole, C., Rothman, K.J. (1990). Epidemiologic science and public health policy. *Journal of Clinical Epidemiology, 43*, 1270.

Rawls, J. (1971). *A Theory of Justice*. Cambridge, Massachusetts: Belknap Press.

Rothman, K. J., Poole, C. (1985). Science and policy making. *American Journal of Public Health, 75*, 340–341.

Weed, D.L. (1994). Science, ethics guidelines, and advocacy in epidemiology. *Annals of Epidemiology, 4*, 166–171.

Index

ACT UP, 42, 162
Action, 1, 2, 4, 9, 12, 43, 49, 64, 65, 66, 69, 73, 75, 77, 81, 82, 83, 84, 87, 89, 90, 108, 125, 136, 149, 150, 162
Action plan, 47, 66
Action research, 2
Acquired immune deficiency syndrome (AIDS), 12
ADA: see Americans with Disabilities Act
Administrative law, 79, 92, 93, 94, 97, 102
Administrative Procedure Act, 93
Advocacy, 6, 10, 11, 12, 13, 46–58, 72–74, 76, 77, 79, 80, 81, 83, 84, 85, 87, 89, 90, 101, 102, 120, 133, 135, 139, 140, 145, 159
  defined, 39, 116
Alcohol, 50, 61, 76, 86–88, 89, 90, 122, 133, 137, 146, 147, 153
  and driving,124, 148–150, 152
Alinsky, Saul, 40, 41
Alliance Against Intoxicated Motorists, 50, 87
Alliance Healthcare Foundation, 10, 135, 153
American Academy of Pediatrics, 73
American Cancer Society, 72
American College of Obstetricians and Gynecologists, 73, 75
American Lung Association, 71
American Nurses Association, 73
American Psychological Organization, 52
Americans with Disabilities Act, 109
Anthropology, 4, 7, 25, 143

Ballot initiative, 71, 89
Beneficence, 159

Bill of attainder, 80
Bill of Rights, 78
Boost Alcohol Consciousness Concerning the Health of University Students, (BACCHUS), 50, 87
Brady Campaign, 48, 51
Brady Center to Prevent Gun Violence, 48

California Association of Hospitals and Health Systems, 72
California Environmental Quality Act, 110
California Medical Association, 72
Casa en Casa, 51
Causal relationships, 29, 143
Census, 22, 23, 112
Centers for Disease Control and Prevention, 18, 23, 114, 132, 153
Children, 73, 85, 87, 107, 109, 113, 114, 117, 151
Children's National Medical Center, 73
Civil law, 76, 78, 103, 105
Class action lawsuits, 106
Clean Air Act of 1990, 96
Cloture, 82
Coalition, 42, 52, 53, 84, 100, 102, 134, 139, 149, 164
  external factors, 63
  internal factors, 71
  requisite elements, 63
Coalition for a Healthy California, 71
Code of Federal Regulations, 96
Collaboration, 65
Communitarian philosophy, 7, 8
Community, 4, 11, 43, 46, 87, 119, 126, 132, 134, 136, 137, 139, 143, 147, 150

Community (*cont.*)
  defined, 1, 2, 3, 160
    anthropology, 4, 7
    of circumstance, 4, 5, 161
    communitarian philosophy, 7, 8
    disease status, 9, 10, 161
    geographic, 3–12
    of crisis, 8
    of ideas, 5, 8
    of interest, 3–7
    of memory, 8
    psychology, 6, 7
    public health, 1, 2, 7, 9, 10
    sociology, 3, 4, 6, 7
  formation of, 4, 5
  organization of, 7, 12
  readiness,11, 161
  sense of, 5–10, 161
  virtual, 2, 3
Community mobilization, 43, 137, 139, 145,
    152
Community organization theory, 40, 41
Community organizing, 6, 22, 39, 121, 134
  defined, 41
  grassroots approaches, 42, 43
Community Trials Project, 152
Conflict of interest, 55, 162, 163
Congress, 11, 55, 74, 90, 92, 93, 96, 97
Constitution, 77–81, 89, 95, 149
Constructivism, 143
Content analysis, 146
Criminal law, 78

Dangerous Promises Campaign, 119
Data analysis, 19, 21, 22, 25, 28, 144
  content analysis, 146
  thematic analysis, 29
Data coding, 29
Data collection, 20, 21, 23, 25, 141, 144
  primary, 31
  questionnaire, 24, 25, 26
  secondary, 19
Databases, 21, 23
De Madres a Madres, 70, 71, 76
Delphi technique, 26
Department of Health and Human
    Services, 74, 79, 141
Deposition, 106
Depression, 34, 53
Discovery, 106

Dissemination, 22, 56, 75, 94, 148
Domestic violence, 105, 114, 135, 163
Drug Use Forecasting System, 33
Drunken driving, 147

Education for Critical Consciousness, 40
Empowerment, 38–40, 46, 48, 53, 63, 76,
    137
Engrossed bill, 82
Enrolled bill, 82
Environmental justice, 112, 113, 117, 118
Environmental Protection Agency, 23, 110,
    112
Ethics, 134, 136, 159
Ethnographic interviews, 24
Evaluation, 11, 23, 31, 64, 69, 136, 137, 141
  types of, 142
    formative, 11, 141
    impact, 142
    outcome, 141
    process, 105, 107, 110, 111, 112, 115, 141
Evaluation data, 31, 142
  qualitative, 21, 110, 142
  quantitative, 21, 143
Evaluation paradigms, 143
  constructivism, 143
  feminist methods, 144
  interpretivism, 143
  participatory, 144
  theory-based, 145
Ex post facto laws, 81

Family Life Development Center, 51
Federal Insecticide, Fungicide, and
    Rodenticide Act, 100
Federal Register, 79, 100
Filibuster, 82
Focus groups, 21, 24, 26, 27, 154
  advantages, 27
  disadvantages, 27
  facilitating, 27
  guide, 21
  size, 27
Food and Drug Administration (FDA), 56,
    77, 79, 92
Formative evaluation, 141, 154
Formative research, 11, 12, 141
Freire, Paolo, 40, 41
Funding, 20, 28, 29, 30, 34, 65, 85, 88, 162

Group interviews, 22, 26, 27
Guidelines, 25, 26, 38, 47, 79, 134

Harm reduction, 10, 13, 33, 34, 44
Healthy Mothers, Healthy Babies
    Coalition, 73–76
Hepatitis B, 30, 32
House of Representatives, 79, 81, 82, 92
Houston, Texas, 70
Human immunodeficiency virus (HIV), 7,
    9, 10, 11, 12, 58, 105, 108, 109, 133, 137,
    160, 163; *see also* Acquired immune
    deficiency syndrome (AIDS)

Indigenous community organizer, 45
Indigent health care, 48, 49, 50, 51, 70
Individual interviews, 21, 23, 27, 28
Informal interviews, 24
Informed consent, 33, 77, 162
Injection drug use, 7, 9, 10, 12, 13, 33, 153,
    154, 161, 163
Injury, 47, 51, 73, 74, 76
Intentionality, 64
Interpretivism, 143
Interviews, 2, 21–23, 26, 28, 29, 30, 34, 135,
    142
    cost, 26
    ethnographic, 24
    groups, 26
    guides, 33
    individual, 23, 28
    informal, 24
    key informant, 24
    semi-structured, 24, 32
    structured, 24, 25, 145
    telephone, 25, 26, 152
    time, 32
    unstructured, 24, 145

Joint Commission on Mental Illness and
    Health, 52
Jurisdiction, 11, 79, 80, 81 150
Justice, 87, 112, 113, 117, 118, 123, 126, 148, 160

Key informant interviews, 24

Lead, 4, 64, 99, 113
Leadership, 5, 38, 41, 45, 50, 56, 61, 64, 65,
    66, 67, 68, 70, 71, 72, 73, 74, 88, 124
Leukemia, 113, 117

Liberating dialogue, 41
Lobbyists, 83, 84, 154

MADD: *see* Mothers Against Drunk
    Driving
March of Dimes, 70
Marches, 47, 108, 109
Maryland Cancer Consortium, 100
Media, 5, 12, 44, 47, 48, 50, 51, 53, 55, 73,
    84, 85, 87, 88, 89, 90, 101, 107, 109,
    114, 117, 124, 130, 135
Media advocacy, 89, 90, 119, 121, 123, 135,
    139, 145
    audience, 122, 128, 132, 140, 149
    elements, 121, 145
    events, 123, 126, 131, 135, 137, 146, 150
    message, 108, 122, 125, 129, 131, 133, 141,
    154
    method, 122, 145
Medical records, 30, 31, 33
Membership, 6, 55, 73, 134, 150, 160
Mental illness, 73, 51–54, 101
Mental retardation, 90
Methodology
    qualitative, 21
    quantitative, 21
Milk, 151
Million Mom March, 44, 48
Moral Crusade, 44
Mothers Against Drunk Driving, 44, 48,
    50, 85, 87, 88, 89, 90, 124, 137 147,
    148, 149

NAMI: *see* National Alliance for the
    Mentally Ill
National Alliance for the Mentally Ill, 51,
    53, 54
National Coalition for Cancer
    Survivorship, 47, 51
National Committee for Mental Hygiene,
    44, 51, 52
National Congress of Parents and
    Teachers, 74
National Council of La Raza, 18
National Institute of Mental Health, 54
National Mental Health Association, 51, 52,
    53, 72
National Mental Health Foundation, 52
National Organization for Mentally Ill
    Children, 52

National SAFE KIDS Campaign, 73
NCCS: *see* National Coalition for Cancer
    Survivorship
Need, 4, 6 10, 11, 13, 62, 84, 152
    defined, 19
Needle exchange, 31–34, 126, 161, 163; *see
    also* Syringe exchange
Needs assessment, 34, 165
    credibility, 88–89
    data, 21
        epidemiological, 30
        interviews, 126, 129
        literature, 62, 119
        medical records, 30
        surveys, 31, 32
    defined, 17–19
    stages, 20
        assessment, 70
        post-assessment, 22
        pre-assessment, 23
    uses, 27
    validity, 20
New York City, 7, 57, 109, 117, 131
NMHA, 137; *see also* National Mental
    Health Association
Nominal group technique, 26
Nonmaleficence, 161
Notice and comment procedures, 95, 96, 97

Occupational Safety and Health
    Administration, 99
Orange County Task Force on Indigent
    Health Care, 48, 49, 50, 51, 70
Organizational capacity, 64, 65, 68

Pacific Institute for Community
    Organizations (PICO), 39
Participatory evaluation, 143, 144
Participatory research, 2
Pocket veto, 83
Policy memoranda, 79
Post-assessment, 22
Post-modern theory, 40, 42
Power, 43, 48, 49, 50, 58, 80, 81, 98, 103,
    104, 105, 113, 144, 160
Pre-assessment, 21, 23, 26
Prenatal care, 70
Presidential veto, 83
Press release, 58, 127, 128, 131, 132
Preventable injury, 73

Priority setting process, 128
Private law, 77, 78
Program evaluation, 23, 153
Pro-Youth Coalition, 69
Protection motivation theory, 120
Psychiatric Foundation, 51, 52
Psychology, 6, 7, 52, 76
Public education, 10, 11, 13, 34, 53
Public health, 1, 2, 7, 9–11, 33, 39, 44, 63,
    74–76, 112, 114, 121, 122, 133, 136, 153,
    154, 155, 160
Public law, 77
Public service advertisements, 128

Questionnaires, 20, 24, 25, 26, 32

Rallies, 47, 108
Reflection, 39, 40, 50
Refugees, 34
Regulations, 77, 100, 101
Rehabilitation Act of 1973, 109
Reliability, 20, 25, 34
    interview data, 146
    needs assessment, 20
Remove Intoxicated Drivers, 50, 87
Reporters, 124, 125, 126
Res judicata, 80
Research, 1, 2, 6, 7, 9, 10–12, 34, 49, 70, 72,
    76, 84, 85, 86, 99, 104, 106, 107, 146,
    150, 160
Resource allocation, 18, 19
Response rates, 25
Rulemaking, 100
    formal, 93
    informal, 93, 97
    negotiated, 95
Rules, 7, 77, 79
    interpretive, 96
    legislative, 96
    substantive, 96

SADD: *see* Students Against Drunk
    Driving
Safe Drinking Water Act, 100
Sampling, 20, 25
San Diego, California, 10, 11, 12, 13, 29, 153,
    154, 155, 161
Self-defense, 115, 116
Semi-structured interviews, 24
Small group, 28, 41, 46, 47

Smoking, 72, 101
The Snake Pit, 52, 120
Social marketing, 123, 132, 151
Social movement, 40, 42, 54, 57, 84
Sociology, 3, 4, 6, 7
Special interest groups, 83–85
Special rule, 82
Stakeholders, 21, 27, 53, 143, 144, 161
Stare decisis, 80
Statutes, 77, 78, 80
Stipends, 33
Story, 76, 119, 124, 126, 127, 135, 136, 140
Strategic communications, 139, 140
Structural capacity, 67
Structured interviews, 23, 24, 25
Students Against Drunk Driving, 50, 87
Substance abuse, 30, 31, 34, 61, 62, 145, 155, 165
Survey, 30, 31, 32, 33, 84, 122, 142, 147, 148, 151, 152
Syringe exchange, 30, 31, 32, 34, 136
    basis for, 10, 145, 153, 154, 155
    cost, 30
    needs assessment, 30, 154, 155
    prevention of disease, 11, 13, 145, 154
    San Diego County, 10, 11, 13, 33, 153, 155, 161

Target population, 10, 19, 21, 25, 26, 27, 28, 29, 30, 70, 141, 160

Target population (*cont.*)
    defining, 1
Technical capacity, 67
Telephone interviews, 25, 26, 153
Tenderloin Senior Organizing Project, 46, 51
Texas Women's University, 70
Theory-based evaluation, 145
Tobacco, 101, 150
Torrington, Connecticut, 115
Town hall meeting, 26, 46, 47, 57
Trials, 122
    clinical, 10, 102
    legal, 81, 89
Triangulation, 21, 22
TSOP: *see* Tenderloin Senior Organizing Project

Unstructured interviews, 24

Validity, 25, 54, 161
    interview data, 146
    needs assessments, 54
Values, 4, 5, 7, 8, 19, 49, 69, 126, 160
Vinyl chloride, 99, 102

Warren County, North Carolina, 112
Wetlands Act, 113
Woburn, Massachusetts, 113
Worcester AIDS Consortium, 71, 76
Writ of certiorari, 104